THROUGH THE YEAR WITH NEWMAN

Through the Year with Newman

Daily Readings

EDITED BY BERNARD DIVE

burns & oates

Published by Burns & Oates
A Continuum Imprint

The Tower Building
11 York Road
London
SE1 7NX

80 Maiden Lane
Suite 704
New York
NY 10038

www.continuumbooks.com

Essay 'Reading Newman' and selection and arrangement of
Newman extracts © Bernard Dive, 2012

First published 2012

British Library Cataloguing-in-Publication Data
A catalogue record for this book is available from the British Library.

ISBN: PB: 978-0-8264-3919-2

Typeset by Fakenham Prepress Solutions, Fakenham, Norfolk NR21 8NN
Printed and bound in India

Contents

Acknowledgements

Extracts from the 'Oratory Papers' of John Henry Newman, first published in *Newman the Oratorian* ed. by Placid Murray (Leominster: Fowler Wright, 1968), are quoted by kind permission of the Birmingham Oratory.

Abbreviations

Apo.	*Apologia pro Vita Sua*
AR	*Addresses to Cardinal Newman and his Replies*
Ari.	*The Arians of the Fourth Century*
CF	*The Church of the Fathers*
CS	*Catholic Sermons of Cardinal Newman*
DA	*Discussions and Arguments on Various Subjects*
Dev.	*An Essay on the Development of Christian Doctrine*
Diff.	*Certain Difficulties felt by Anglicans in Catholic Teaching*
Ess.	*Essays Critical and Historical*
GA	*An Essay in Aid of a Grammar of Assent*
HS	*Historical Sketches*
Idea	*The Idea of a University*
Jfc.	*Lectures on the Doctrine of Justification*
LES	*Lives of the English Saints*
MD	*Meditations and Devotions of the late Cardinal Newman*
Mir.	*Two Essays on Biblical and on Ecclesiastical Miracles*
Mix.	*Discourses addressed to Mixed Congregations*
OP	'Oratory Papers', in *Newman the Oratorian*
OS	*Sermons Preached on Various Occasions*
Prepos.	*The Present Position of Catholics in England*
PS	*Parochial and Plain Sermons*
SD	*Sermons bearing on Subjects of the Day*
SN	*Sermon Notes of John Henry Cardinal Newman*
US	*Fifteen Sermons preached before the University of Oxford*
VM	*The Via Media*
VV	*Verses on Various Occasions*

All excerpts are taken from the Longman, Green, and Co. uniform edition of the works of Newman, except for those from *Catholic Sermons of Cardinal Newman* ed. by Fathers of the Birmingham Oratory (London: Burns & Oates, 1957), *Sermon Notes of John Henry Cardinal Newman* ed. by Fathers of the Birmingham Oratory (London, 1913) and from the 'Oratory Papers', in *Newman the Oratorian* ed. by Placid Murray (Leominster: Fowler Wright, 1968).

In all references, roman numerals refer to volume numbers, Arabic numerals to chapters, sections and subsections within volumes.

Reading Newman

John Henry Newman is a good Christian thinker to live with because he is concerned with Christian belief as something to live out. For Newman, the Christian revelation, the 'Divine Word', is 'with power'; the 'ideas which Christianity brings before us are in themselves full of influence' and in forming the mind and character they inform the way in which one lives.[1] It is no accident that he is best known for his *Apologia pro Vita Sua* (1864) in which he relates the development of his religious opinions – the story of how he went from Evangelicalism to Anglo Catholicism to Roman Catholicism – by giving a picture of the activity over time of 'that living intelligence, by which I write, and argue, and act'.[2] For Newman, 'intelligence' was not something apart from life, and ideas that were not 'living' were of little value.

The distinctiveness of Newman as a thinker comes from his attentiveness to the personal and concrete dimensions of thought, to the ways in which individuals – acted upon by their 'hopes, fears, and existing opinions' – accept or reject the ideas presented to them in everyday life.[3] He lived at a time when considerable efforts had been made to consider the 'evidences' for Christianity – to isolate the proofs of Christian doctrine and to arrange those proofs according to strictly logical criteria – and his response was to note that such proofs had little to do with actual faith, with the real motives for belief. Christians are not brought to faith by elaborate reasoning, in which assent is carefully proportioned to the evidence, but by a response to the 'Divine Word' in which the whole person is engaged.

That belief does not rely on orderly logical formulae need not mean that to believe is to go against reason. When one must act, it is reasonable to make do with imperfect proofs. If the Christian revelation is meant to affect everyday life, and is addressed to

1

individuals in the midst of the world – if, that is, it is addressed to the practical and moral intellect – then it is only proper that it should act on the mind in this way, for 'man is *not* a reasoning animal; he is a seeing, feeling, contemplating, acting animal'.[4] This is not to say that those who accept Christianity do not have reasons for doing so, but that their reasoning need not be brought out into explicit form: 'all men have a reason, but not all men can give a reason'.[5] Reasoning is the natural, spontaneous work of the mind. The formal notation of logic – 'paper logic' – is copied from (and verified against) this natural activity.[6] 'Paper logic', rather than being an instrument of thought, is merely the record of it, wrought out in a secondary process in which the mind reflects on its own activity: it can serve a negative function, in testing arguments for consistency; but it does not create the vision of reality that one must live by.

For Newman, then, to make sense of how individuals come to accept Christianity is to examine the movement of the living mind. To recognize that the Christian revelation has a power proceeding from the work of the Spirit – that the 'ideas' of Christianity are 'attended with a supernatural gift over and above themselves' – is not to reject the possibility of making some sense of this power by looking at the natural workings of the mind.[7] 'God influences us and works in us through our minds, not without them or in spite of them.'[8] The agency of the Creator does not compete with or cancel out the agency of the creature. An acute, sensitive and patient attentiveness to the delicate movements of the mind informed the greatest achievements of Newman as a thinker: his *Sermons Preached before the University of Oxford* (1843) sought to characterize how people actually believe; his *Essay on the Development of Christian Doctrine* (1845) interpreted the history of the Church, and its accumulation of dogmas over the centuries, as an expression of the way in which ideas live in the intellect, with their manifold aspects being brought out, over time, spontaneously; his *Essay in Aid of a Grammar of Assent* (1870) analysed the ways in which the mind works in entertaining and accepting ideas, and the differences between conceptual and imaginative apprehension. Newman did not attempt to portray, in all its fullness and fluidity, the natural life of the mind – for 'no analysis is subtle and delicate enough to represent adequately the state of mind under which we believe, or the subjects of belief as they are presented to our thoughts' – but he sought to evoke it, to characterize it, and to insist on its complexity.[9] He insisted that not every way to truth could be reduced to rule.

Newman felt that religious belief is a love of the God revealed to the conscience. Faith in Christianity arises from the experience of seeing in the Christian revelation a manifestation of the God already encountered in the 'voice' of conscience, and a satisfaction of the longings aroused by efforts to live by the conscience.

Newman sees the conscience as an awareness of right and wrong with respect to particular, concrete actions. The work of the conscience is not primarily a matter of consulting and applying explicit rules or principles; rather, it is a matter of deciding whether a particular action, here and now, should be carried out. While principles can be inferred from the particular deliverances of the conscience, and can be invoked in deliberations about what one should do, such principles are too abstract to be fully adequate to the complexities presented by a concrete situation. Ultimately, one must decide what to do in particular situations, bringing to the decision all that one is. Taking cognizance of explicit rules is a part of what is involved in making the decision, but not the whole. The conscience, then, is eminently personal (and, indeed, the enuncia- tions of the conscience will vary from person to person); but what is universal about the experience of obeying the conscience is, precisely, the experience of obedience: of being commanded. As such, the conscience presents itself as 'more than a man's own self' and it 'carries on our minds to a Being exterior to ourselves ... [and] superior to ourselves', to a God who, as the origin of a good law, unlimited in its claims, is revealed to be infinitely good.[10] Newman suggests that 'natural religion' – that is to say, the religion of those who have not encountered the explicit revelation of Christianity – arises from trying to obey the conscience: in making this effort, one experiences God as present yet remote, a hidden God, and one realizes that one is remote from God in being unable to fulfil the commands of the conscience adequately. For Newman, the history of the religions of the world exhibits an unappeased longing for atonement. When one tries to obey the conscience, one comes to an awareness of the need for grace: the effort creates a predisposition to accept the assistance offered by God in Christianity. When one tries to obey the conscience, one comes to an ever clearer sense of the holiness of God: the effort creates a predisposition to accept that assistance from God is likely, is consistent with His goodness.

Christianity is, then, an eminently practical matter. The Christian revelation is addressed to those who are trying, as best they can, to live well. Those who are making this effort will be predisposed to believe the Christian revelation, because it answers to their needs; and the reasoning involved in their acceptance of its claims will be the reasoning of practical life (not a series of perfectly articulated syllogisms). In his approach to the understanding of religious thought, Newman vindicated the ways in which ordinary Christians think. To justify Christianity, one need not form an elaborate theory or system of proof; one need only observe how faith comes into being in everyday life. (If there is a God, and if the providence of God governs the world, then one can suppose that the ways in which people do come to believe in God – whatever the formal 'correctness' of these methods – are sanctioned by God; and, in any case, a questioning of the human faculty to know can only be taken so far: at a certain point, one is simply obliged to use what one has, what one is.) Newman respected everyday Christian faith because he believed that Christianity was meant to act on the world, and that one test of the validity of a mode of presenting Christianity, and of Christian doctrine, was whether or not it worked.

Newman had pastoral duties for most of his life, and felt his responsibilities, as one tasked with the care of souls, keenly. In his parochial work, Newman could see Christianity becoming an everyday reality, transforming and sustaining lives; and he could, moreover, see all the forces that hindered it from being properly acted upon. One of his abiding preoccupations in assessing ideas was whether or not those ideas were 'real'. For an idea to be 'real', it had to correspond to reality and it had to be possible to live by it; and to be real as a person, one had to live by what one professed: indeed, one could tell what people really believed by what they did. 'That a thing is true, is no reason that it should be said, but that it should be done; that it should be acted upon; that it should be made our own inwardly.'[11] Acting upon an idea, and assimilating it 'inwardly', were different aspects of the same process. The respect of Newman for the faith of ordinary Christians was deepened by his scholarly researches into the history of the Church: in the fourth century, when the Arian heresy – maintaining that

Christ was not God, but a creature – was dividing the Church, the orthodox faith was attested more by the actions of the laity than by the teaching of the official leaders of the Church. This historical interlude showed, Newman felt, the value of the *sensus fidelium*, the faith of ordinary believers whose prophetical office was bestowed on them by their baptism: 'the body of the faithful is one of the witnesses to the fact of the tradition of revealed doctrine, and ... their *consensus* through Christendom is the voice of the Infallible Church'.[12]

To recognize that Christianity is something to be lived out is not to claim that Christian faith could be explained by, and reduced to, its effects on the lives of those who accept it. To do so would be to 'rationalize' – to propose a function for the Christian revelation that the intellect can clearly comprehend, and to refer everything in the revelation to that function. Newman discerned a tendency in his time for people to see religion as a matter of 'sentiment' and to interpret Christianity as something designed to procure moral effects, to shape the emotions and character; and he believed that this tendency resulted in a willingness to discard anything from traditional Christianity that could not be shown to serve a moral purpose. Newman insisted on the objective and mysterious character of the revelation – mysterious because objective, because the revelation of a God whose perfection was beyond comprehension: 'no revelation can be complete and systematic, from the weakness of the human intellect'.[13] To those who considered the obscurity of the revelation to mar its credibility, Newman replied that such obscurity was consistent with a revelation of a transcendent God, and that, moreover, one should not suppose that the revelation was intended to satisfy a desire for knowledge ('grace ... is given, not that we may know more, but that we may do better').[14] To those inclined to explain the revelation wholly in reference to our efforts to 'do better', Newman replied that the revelation was a revelation of God through Christ – the revelation of a Divine Object – that it was not possible to ascertain how the revelation affected us – to discern which parts of it had a 'moral' effect and which did not – and that to separate an emotional response from the object to which it was a response was 'a dream and a mockery': 'as well can there be filial love without the fact of a father, as devotion without the fact of a Supreme Being'.[15]

Much of the power of Newman as a thinker comes from his awareness of the personal dimension of thought: his awareness of how, when matters of ultimate concern are in question, the whole person is engaged. Much of his power as a preacher and theologian comes from his sense of Christianity as creating a new way of being a person: an existence animated by the indwelling of the Holy Spirit in the soul. For Newman, Christianity is 'at once a philosophy, a political power, and a religious rite', and to see it accurately is to see in all these forms the expression of a unitary life.[16] This life is the expression of the Christian 'idea', a vision of the action of God in the world through Christ, an idea which, realizing itself over the course of time by a natural process, has developed into a 'religious rite' and a 'political power'; yet if this process is natural, it is simultaneously supernatural, the expression of a divine life: the work of the Spirit in the world, and a 'portion' of the 'unseen world [that] through God's secret power and mercy, encroaches upon this world'.[17]

All Christians, by virtue of their baptism, receive the presence of the Spirit in the soul, which 'pervades [them] ... as light pervades a building, or as a sweet perfume the folds of some honourable robe'[18] and which unites them to the Risen Christ, whereby 'they are one and all the births and manifestations of one and the same unseen spiritual principle or power, "*living* stones," internally connected, as branches from a tree, not as the parts of a heap ... their separate persons being but as separate developments, vessels, instruments, and works of Him who is invisible'.[19] Christians become holy by being united to Christ; and this union transforms every aspect of their lives: as God in Christ assumed human existence in its entirety, conferring on it His own holiness, so everyday human existence – however humdrum – can become a work of the highest holiness.

Newman sees Christian existence as profoundly mysterious: there is more in it – a secret divine presence – than is immediately apparent. When one is attempting to assess the way in which the Christian revelation affects those to whom it is presented, one can examine the natural mental processes involved, but one should be aware of what is 'superadded to earth from heaven': 'Christianity differs from other religions and philosophies ... not in kind, but in origin; not in its nature, but in its personal characteristics; being informed and quickened by what is more than intellect,

by a divine spirit'.[20] The spirit that is 'more than intellect' works
through the intellect – and indeed through all of human life – so
that the activity of the intellect becomes something sacramental:
mediating a divine power and presence that transcends it. (It is
an awareness of the sacramental power of the revelation that
should make one zealous to preserve every aspect of it, however
mysterious: doctrines that seem otiose might have an undetected
effect or importance.) The element in Christianity 'superadded
to earth from heaven' could show itself in more-than-natural
effects – in miraculous phenomena – but it could equally (and did
ordinarily) work through everyday occurrences. Newman insisted
on the mysteriousness of the usual. It is, he believed, 'our duty' to
contemplate God not only 'in heaven' but 'in our hearts and souls',
'viewing by faith His glory without and within us', and 'acting
towards and for Him in the works of every day'.[21] If Christianity,
even in its most mysterious aspects, is something addressed to
everyday life, so everyday life is revealed by Christianity to be
mysterious.

Christians should be astonished at themselves, because they
have within them a 'spiritual principle ... so great, so wondrous,
that all the powers in the visible world, all the conceivable forces
and appetites of matter, all the physical miracles which are at this
day in process of discovery, almost superseding time and space,
dispensing with numbers, and rivalling mind, all these powers of
nature are nothing to this gift within us'.[22] One should not look to
see this 'spiritual principle' as manifesting itself in unusual actions
or states of mind; its presence is shown in unremarkable acts of
goodness; its work – in altering the condition of the soul – is
hidden because the condition of the soul is hidden. One should not
contemplate oneself – except to acknowledge how far one is from
perfection – but one should look to Christ, and try, from moment
to moment, to act rightly: 'he who aims vaguely and generally
at being in a spiritual frame of mind, is entangled in a deceit of
words'.[23] To see how the presence of the Spirit in the soul can bring
about a holy life, one can look to the saints: the 'triumph of the
Gospel' is that it has 'made men saints, and brought into existence
specimens of faith and holiness, which without it are unknown and
impossible'; but in trying to realize holiness, one should simply try
to fulfil the duties 'of every day'.[24] The most famous of the poems
of Newman, 'Lead kindly light', articulates this spirituality of

alertness to the requirements of the moment: 'I do not ask to see /
The distant scene – one step enough for me.'[25]

Newman did not envisage faith as possessing a clear sight of
'the distant scene', of the secrets of God. Faith provides the best
possible sight of those secrets, but it is not a full sight: the divine
life remains obscure, beyond comprehension. 'Religious Truth is
neither light nor darkness, but both together; it is like the dim view
of a country seen in the twilight, with forms half extricated from
the darkness, with broken lines, and isolated masses.'[26] Faith, like
conscience, is a matter of gaining enough sight to live by, to take
the next 'step'; and, with each 'step' taken, more light is given.
Yet Newman believed that faith could develop into 'wisdom' or
'philosophy' – a larger view of things acquired through reflection
on the knowledge sustaining a holy life. To reflect on the whole
of reality is to see particular things more clearly – to avoid partial
views – and a wisdom of this kind 'makes every thing lead to every
thing else; it communicates the image of the whole body to every
separate member, till the whole becomes in imagination like a
spirit, every where pervading and penetrating its component parts,
and giving them their one definite meaning'.[27] If there is anything
that gives the preaching and devotional writing of Newman its
signal force, it is his capacity to bring to the consideration of any
particular topic an awareness of the unity and consistency of the
Christian faith, and to discern particular questions in relation to
the whole Christian revelation: it is his wisdom.

His openness to making 'every thing lead to every thing else'
prompted him to coordinate all the knowledge he possessed, to
connect Christian doctrine with secular knowledge: 'it will not
satisfy me ... to have two independent systems, intellectual and
religious, going at once side by side'.[28] He was not satisfied by
a disjunction of religious from secular knowledge because each
form of knowledge would be impoverished by the separation,
and because he considered the perfection of the intellect – the
aim of liberal education – to be a good in itself (albeit not the
highest good). In his sermons, he brought a rich awareness of the
nature of human life – acquired through intensely apprehended
personal experience and extensive reading – to the interpretation
of Scripture, probing the bare and enigmatic narratives of the Bible
to infer the motives and characteristics of the protagonists, and
then turning from the text to apply the knowledge obtained from

it to the circumstances of his own time. In this work of application there was a bringing together of disparate forms of knowledge to discern something universal: the 'drama of religion, and the combat of truth and error', which, occurring in a wide variety of different historical circumstances, is nevertheless 'ever one and the same'.[29]

Newman sought to see the 'drama of religion' in and through the circumstances of his time – to see the world as the 'scene of a higher conflict', glimpsing the higher world through the 'thick black veil … spread between this world and the next' – and he endeavoured to present his vision of this drama in an emotionally compelling manner.[30] If he tried to orient himself towards eternity, he was nevertheless aware that eternity presents itself in the duties of life; and almost everything he wrote (the most notable exception being his *Essay in Aid of a Grammar of Assent*) was written to discharge obligations of the moment – whether his sermons, in which, working with and through the given Scriptural 'text' of the day, he sought to provide for the needs of his congregation, or his controversial writings, where he sought to address the problems of his time. While most of his writings are 'occasional', they arise from a perception of the requirements of the immediate occasion in relation to the unchanging truth of God, a view of the moment in relation to the whole.

How should one read Newman? How would he want to be read? He was suspicious of forms of devotional reading that issued only in a 'luxury of excited religious feeling, in a mere meditating on our Blessed Lord, and dwelling as in a reverie on what He has done for us'. Though he wrote a couple of novels, he was ambivalent about the value of fiction: in reading a novel 'we have nothing *to do*; we read, are affected, softened or roused, and that is all' but 'God has made us feel in order that we may *go on to act* in consequence of feeling; if then we allow our feelings to be excited without acting upon them, we do mischief to the moral system within us, just as we might spoil a watch, or other piece of mechanism, by playing with the wheels of it.'[31]

Newman considered Christianity – as a form of life, not a mere theory – to be spread more by personal relationships and influences than by books. In his *Apologia pro Vita Sua*, he dwelt on the friendships that he considered to have been relevant to the development of his opinions. Even his account, in the *Apologia*, of an experience of reading that profoundly affected his opinions – the experience of meditating on a phrase from the writings of Saint Augustine, '*securus judicat orbis terrarum*' – is framed by an acknowledgement of how the passage in question was pointed out to him by a 'friend, an anxiously religious man, now, as then, very dear to me.'[32] Newman shows how the phrase from Saint Augustine acquires a unique, personal meaning for him; and he shows the situation in which it does so: a situation of personal relationships and friendships. There is something incalculable about the way the text is received, about how it acts upon life. For Newman, even the most authoritative of books – the Scriptures – could not be seen as a repository of the whole truth of Christianity, because 'ideas are in the writer and reader of the revelation, not the inspired text itself'.[33] There is more in the minds of 'writer and reader' than can be contained in a 'text'. The New Testament records ideas that arose from a personal encounter with an individual, with Jesus: ideas that existed in a living tradition before being committed to writing and that have been, and will be, expressed in all the authentic actions of the Church, the community of those whose lives are formed by the image and memory of Jesus. The Scriptures have, for Newman, unassailable authority, but they are not the only authority. The most perfect disclosure of the truth of God that has been given was not, after all, a book, but a living man.

If Newman was concerned about reading that produced a 'luxury of excited religious feeling' and little else, he nevertheless recognized that meditation was an indispensible part of Christian life: the Christian must 'create within him an image of what is absent', 'realise by faith what he does not see' and must therefore meditate; and meditation could, and should, be a part of an active life – something to be a part of every day of the year: 'think of the Cross when you rise and when you lie down, when you go out and when you come in, when you eat and when you walk and when you converse, when you buy and when you sell, when you labour and when you rest'.[34] Newman can give wisdom for each day because his wisdom addressed itself to the needs of real life. Good reading, for him, was reading that belonged to the discipline of a good life. 'We were made for action, and for right action, – for thought, and for true thought. Let us live while we live; let us be alive and doing.'[35]

Notes

Except for instances where references are made to editions or works not used in compiling this volume, in all references in these notes the same abbreviations are used as have been employed throughout this volume (see p. ix)

1. DA., p. 270.
2. John Henry Newman, *Apologia pro Vita Sua* ed. by Ian Ker (London: Penguin, 1994), p. 436.
3. US, pp. 187–8.
4. DA, p. 294.
5. US, p. 259.
6. Apo., p. 169.
7. DA, p. 270.
8. US, p. 281.
9. US, p. 267.
10. OS, pp. 64–5.
11. PS, v., p. 45.
12. John Henry Newman, *On Consulting the Faithful in Matters of Doctrine*, ed. by John Coulson (London: Geoffrey Chapman, 1961), p. 63.
13. Ess., i, p. 41.
14. PS, i, p. 203.
15. Apo., p. 49.
16. VM, i, p. xl.
17. PS, iv, p. 178.
18. PS, ii, p. 222.
19. PS, iv, p. 170.
20. Dev., p. 57.
21. PS., iii, p. 269.
22. PS, v, p. 345.
23. PS, ii, p. 160.
24. PS, iv, p. 156.
25. VV, p. 156.
26. Ess., i, pp. 41–2.
27. US, p. 291.
28. OS, p. 13.
29. Apo., p. 115.
30. PS, iv, p. 208, PS, v, 10.

31. PS, ii, p. 373, p. 371.
32. Apo., p. 116.
33. Dev., p. 36.
34. PS, v, p. 339.
35. DA, p. 214.

Moveable Feasts

Baptism of the Lord

Christ is Righteousness in God's sight; He is the Well-beloved Son, in whom the Father is well pleased, as being "the Brightness of His glory, and the express Image of His Person," "the unspotted Mirror of the power of God, and the Image of His goodness." Nothing can He absolutely delight in, but what is like Himself; hence he is said to "put no trust even in His servants, and to charge His Angels with folly." None but the Eternal Son, who is incommunicably like the Father, can be infinitely acceptable to Him or simply righteous. Yet in proportion as rational beings are like the Son, or partake of His excellence, so are they really righteous; in proportion as God sees His Son in them, He is well pleased with them ... Christ's righteousness, which is given us, makes us righteous.

Jfc., 5

Ash Wednesday

Fasting is only one branch of a large and momentous duty, the subdual of ourselves to Christ. We must surrender to Him all we have, all we are. We must keep nothing back.

CS, 5

Good Friday

I see One dropping blood, gashed by the thong, and stretched upon the Cross, and He is God ... The Word and Wisdom of the Father, who dwelt in His bosom in bliss ineffable from all eternity, whose very smile has shed radiance and grace over the whole creation,

13

whose traces I see in the starry heavens and on the green earth, this glorious living God, it is He who looks at me so piteously, so tenderly from the Cross. He seems to say, – I cannot move, though I am omnipotent, for sin has bound Me here. I had had it in mind to come on earth among innocent creatures, more fair and lovely than them all, with a face more radiant than the Seraphim, and a form as royal as that of Archangels, to be their equal yet their God, to fill them with My grace, to receive their worship, to enjoy their company, and to prepare them for the heaven to which I destined them; but, before I carried My purpose into effect, they sinned, and lost their inheritance; and so I come indeed, but come, not in that brightness in which I went forth to create the morning stars and to fill the sons of God with melody, but in deformity and in shame, in sighs and tears, with blood upon My cheek, and with My limbs laid bare and rent. Gaze on Me, O My children, if you will, for I am helpless; gaze on your Maker, whether in contempt, or in faith and love. Here I wait, upon the Cross, the appointed time, the time of grace and mercy; here I wait till the end of the world, silent and motionless, for the conversion of the sinful and the consolation of the just; here I remain in weakness and shame, though I am so great in heaven, till the end, patiently expecting My full catalogue of souls, who, when time is at length over, shall be the reward of My passion and the triumph of My grace to all eternity.

Mix., 15

Holy Saturday

Jesus, when He was nearest to His everlasting triumph, seemed to be farthest from triumphing. When He was nearest upon entering upon His kingdom, and exercising all power in heaven and earth, He was lying dead in a cave of the rock. He was wrapped round in burying-clothes, and confined within a sepulchre of stone, where He was soon to have a glorified spiritual body, which could penetrate all substances, go to and fro quicker than thought, and was about to ascend on high. Make us to trust in thee, O Jesus, that Thou wilt display in us a similar providence. Make us sure, O Lord, that the greater is our distress, the nearer we are to Thee. The more men scorn us, the more Thou dost honour us. The more men insult over us, the higher Thou wilt exalt us. The more they forget us, the more Thou dost keep us in mind. The more they abandon us, the closer Thou wilt bring us to Thyself.

MD, 2, 'Meditations on the Stations of the Cross', 14

Easter

Christ is to us now, just what He was in all His glorious Attributes on the morning of the Resurrection; and we are blessed in knowing it, even more than the women to whom the Angels spoke, according to His own assurance, "Blessed are they that have not seen, and yet have believed" ...

When the Word of Life was manifested in our flesh, the Holy Ghost displayed that creative hand by which, in the beginning, Eve was formed; and the Holy Child, thus conceived by the power of the Highest, was (as the history shows) immortal even in His mortal nature, clear from all infection of the forbidden fruit, so far as to be sinless and incorruptible. Therefore, though He was liable to death, "it was impossible He should be *holden*" of it. Death might overpower, but it could not keep possession; "it had no dominion over Him." (Rom. vi. 9.) He was ... "*the Living* among the dead."

And hence His rising from the dead may be said to have evinced His divine original. He was "*declared* to be the Son of God with power, according to the Spirit of Holiness"; that is, His essential Godhead, "by the resurrection of the dead." (Rom. i. 4.) ... Much more abundant was the manifestation of His Godhead, when He was risen from the dead. Then the Divine Essence streamed forth (so to say) on every side, and environed His Manhood, as in a cloud of glory ... Thus manifested as perfect God and perfect man, in the fulness of His sovereignty, and the immortality of His holiness, He ascended up on high to take possession of His kingdom ...

We must not suppose, that in leaving us He closed the gracious economy of His Incarnation, and withdrew the ministration of His incorruptible Manhood from His work of loving mercy towards us. "The Holy One of God" was ordained, not only to die for us, but also to be "the beginning" of a new "creation" unto holiness, in our sinful race; to refashion soul and body after His own likeness, that they might be "raised up together, and sit together in heavenly places in Christ Jesus." Blessed for ever be His Holy Name! before He went away, He remembered our necessity, and completed His work, bequeathing to us a special mode of approaching Him, a Holy Mystery, in which we receive (we know not how) the virtue of that Heavenly Body, which is the life of all that believe. This is the blessed Sacrament of the Eucharist, in which "Christ is evidently set forth crucified among us;" that we, feasting upon the Sacrifice, may be "partakers of the Divine Nature" ... Christ, in the Scripture phrase, is "formed in us;" that is, the communication is made to us of His new nature, which sanctifies the soul, and makes the body immortal.

PS, ii, 13

Ascension of the Lord

My Lord, I follow Thee up to heaven ... This is the triumph. Earth rises to heaven. I see Thee going up. I see that Form which hung upon the Cross, those scarred hands and feet, that pierced side; they are mounting up to heaven. And the Angels are full of jubilee; the myriads of blessed spirits, which people the glorious expanse, part like the waters to let Thee pass. And the living pavement of God's palaces is cleft in twain, and the Cherubim with flaming swords, who form the rampart of heaven against fallen man, give way and open out, that Thou mayest enter, and Thy saints after Thee. O memorable day!

MD, 3.13.1

Pentecost

It was the great promise of the Gospel, that the Lord of all, who had hitherto manifested himself externally to His servants, should take up His abode in their hearts ... Though He had come in our flesh, so as to be seen and handled, even this was not enough. Still He was external and separate; but after His ascension He descended again by and in His Spirit ... There must indeed be a union between all creatures and their Almighty Creator even for their very existence; for it is said, "In Him we live, and move, and have our being" ... But far higher, more intimate, and more sacred is the indwelling of God in the hearts of His elect people; – so intimate, that compared with it, He may well be said not to inhabit other men at all; His presence being specified as the characteristic privilege of His own redeemed servants.

From the day of Pentecost, to the present time, it has been their privilege, according to the promise, "I will pray the Father, and He shall give you another Comforter, that He may abide with you *for ever*," – for ever: not like the Son of man, who having finished His gracious work went away. Then it is added, "even the *Spirit of Truth*:" that is, He who came for ever, came as a Spirit, and, so coming, did for His own that which the visible flesh and blood of the Son of man, from its very nature, could not do, viz., He came into the souls of all who believe, and taking possession of them, He, being One, knit them all together into one. Christ, by coming in the flesh, provided an external or apparent unity, such as had been under the Law. He formed His Apostles into a visible society; but when He came again in the person of His Spirit, He made them all in a real sense one, not in name only. For they were no longer arranged merely in the form of unity, as the limbs of the dead may be, but they were parts and organs of one unseen power; they really depended upon, and were offshoots of that which was One; their separate persons were taken into a mysterious union with things unseen, were grafted upon and assimilated to the spiritual body of Christ, which is One, even by the Holy Ghost, in whom Christ has come again to us. Thus Christ came, not to make us one, but to die for us: the Spirit came to make us one in Him who had died and was alive, that is, to form the Church.

This then is the special glory of the Christian Church, that its members do not depend merely on what is visible, they are not mere stones of a building, piled one on another, and bound together from without, but they are one and all the births and manifestations of one and the same unseen spiritual principle or power, "*living* stones," internally connected, as branches from a tree, not as the parts of a heap. They are members of the Body of Christ. That divine and adorable Form, which the Apostles saw and handled, after ascending into heaven became a principle of life, a secret origin of existence to all who believe, through the gracious ministration of the Holy Ghost. This is the fruitful Vine, and the rich Olive tree upon and out of which all Saints, though wild and barren by nature, grow, that they may bring forth fruit unto God. So that in a true sense it may be said, that from the day of Pentecost to this hour there has been in the Church but One Holy One, the King of kings, and Lord of lords Himself, who is in all believers, and through whom they are what they are; their separate persons being but as separate developments, vessels, instruments, and works of Him who is invisible.

PS, iv, 11

Holy Trinity, Solemnity

The God of all, who is revealed in the Old Testament, is the Father of a Son from everlasting, called also His Word and Image, of His substance and partaker of all His perfections, and equal to Himself, yet without being separate from Him, but one with Him; and ... from the Father and the Son proceeds eternally the Holy Spirit, who also is of one substance, Divinity, and majesty with Father and Son. Moreover ... the Son or Word is a Person, – that is, is to be spoken of as "He," not "it," and can be addressed; and ... the Holy Ghost also is a Person. Thus God subsists in Three Persons, from everlasting to everlasting; first, God is the Father, next God is the Son, next God is the Holy Ghost; and the Father is not the Son, nor the Son the Holy Ghost, nor the Holy Ghost the Father. And God is Each of these Three, and nothing else; that is, He is either the Father, or the Son, or the Holy Ghost. Moreover, God is as wholly and entirely God in the Person of the Father, as though there were no Son and Spirit; as entirely in that of the Son, as though there were no Spirit and Father; as entirely in that of the Spirit, as though there were no Father and Son. And the Father is God, the Son God, and the Holy Ghost God, while there is but one God; and that without any inequality, because there is but One God, and He is without parts or degrees; though how it is that that same Adorable Essence, indivisible, and numerically One, should subsist perfectly and wholly in Each of Three Persons, no words of man can explain, nor earthly illustration typify.

PS, vi, 24

Body and Blood of Christ, Solemnity

My God, I know well, Thou couldst have saved us at Thy word, without Thyself suffering; but Thou didst choose to purchase us at the price of Thy Blood. I look on Thee, the Victim lifted up on Calvary, and I know and protest that that death of Thine was an expiation for the sins of the whole world. I believe and know, that

Thou alone couldst have offered a meritorious atonement; for it was Thy Divine Nature which gave Thy sufferings worth. Rather then than I should perish according to my deserts, Thou wast nailed to the Tree and didst die.

Such a sacrifice was not to be forgotten. It was not to be – it could not be – a mere event in the world's history, which was to be done and over, and was to pass away except in its obscure, unrecognised effects. If that great deed was what we believe it to be, what we know it is, it must remain present, though past; it must be a standing fact for all times ... Yes, my Lord, though Thou hast left the world, Thou art daily offered up in the Mass; and, though Thou canst not suffer pain and death, Thou dost still subject Thyself to indignity and restraint to carry out to the full Thy mercies towards us. Thou dost humble Thyself daily; for, being infinite, Thou couldst not end Thy humiliation while they existed for whom Thou didst submit to it. So Thou remainest a Priest for ever.

My Lord, I offer Thee myself in turn as a sacrifice of thanksgiving. Thou hast died for me, and I in turn make myself over to Thee ... Enable me to carry out what I profess.

MD, 3.15.1

Sacred Heart of Jesus

O Sacred Heart of Jesus, I adore Thee in the oneness of the Personality of the Second Person of the Holy Trinity. Whatever belongs to the Person of Jesus, belongs therefore to God, and is to be worshipped with that one and the same worship which we pay to Jesus ... My God, my Saviour, I adore Thy Sacred Heart, for that heart is the seat and source of all Thy tenderest human affections for us sinners. It is the instrument and organ of Thy love. It did beat for us. It yearned over us. It ached for us, and for our salvation. It was on fire through zeal, that the glory of God might be manifested in and by us. It is the channel through which has come to us all Thy overflowing human affection, all Thy Divine Charity towards us. All Thy incomprehensible compassion for us, as God and Man, as our Creator and our Redeemer and Judge, has come to us, and comes, in one inseparably mingled stream, through that Sacred Heart. O most Sacred symbol and Sacrament of Love, divine and human, in its fulness, Thou didst save me by Thy divine strength, and Thy human affection, and then at length by that wonder-working blood, wherewith Thou didst overflow.

MD, 3.16

Immaculate Heart of Mary

Holy the womb that bare Him,
Holy the breasts that fed,
But holier still the royal heart
That in his passion bled.

MD, 2, 'The Heart of Mary'

Christ the King

A temporal sovereign makes himself felt by means of his subordinate administrators, who bring his power and will to bear upon every individual of his subjects who personally know him not; the universal Deliverer, long expected, when He came, He too, instead of making and securing subjects by a visible graciousness or majesty, departs; – *but* is found, through His preachers, to have imprinted the Image or idea of Himself in the minds of His subjects individually; and that Image, apprehended and worshipped in individual minds, becomes a principle of association, and a real bond of those subjects one with another, who are thus united to the body by being united to that Image; and moreover that Image, which is their moral life, when they have been already converted, is also the original instrument of their conversion. It is the Image of Him who fulfils the one great need of human nature, the Healer of its wounds, the Physician of the soul, this Image it is which both creates faith, and then rewards it.

GA, 10.3

Holy Family

Sympathy may be called an eternal law, for it is signified or rather transcendentally and archetypically fulfilled in the ineffable mutual love of the Divine Trinity ... When, for our sakes, the Son came on earth and took our flesh, yet He would not live without the sympathy of others. For thirty years He lived with Mary and Joseph and thus formed a shadow of the Heavenly Trinity on earth. O the perfection of that sympathy which existed between the three! Not a look of one, but the other two understood, as expressed, better than if expressed in a thousand words – nay more than understood, accepted, echoed, corroborated. It was like three instruments absolutely in tune which all vibrate when one vibrates, and vibrate either one and the same note, or in perfect harmony … O my soul, thou art allowed to contemplate this union of the three, and to share thyself its sympathy, by faith though not by sight. My God, I believe and know that then a communion of heavenly things was opened on earth which has never been suspended. It is my duty and my bliss to enter into it myself. It is my duty and my bliss to be in tune with that most touching music which then began to sound. Give me that grace which alone can make me hear and understand it, that it may thrill through me. Let the breathings of my soul be with Jesus, Mary, and Joseph. Let me live in obscurity, out of the world and the world's thought, with them. Let me look to them in sorrow and in joy, and live and die in their sweet sympathy.

MD, 3.2.2

General Calendar

January

January 1

Mary, Mother of God, Solemnity

The Blessed Virgin is *Theotocos*, *Deipara*, or Mother of God ... God is her Son, as truly as any one of us is the son of his own mother ... What dignity can be too great to attribute to her who is as closely bound up, as intimately one, with the Eternal Word, as a mother is with a son? What outfit of sanctity, what fulness and redundance of grace, what exuberance of merits must have been hers, when once we admit the supposition ... that her Maker really did regard those merits, and take them into account, when He condescended "not to abhor the Virgin's womb"? Is it surprising then that on the one hand she should be immaculate in her Conception? or on the other that she should be honoured with an Assumption, and exalted as a queen with a crown of twelve stars, with the rulers of day and night to do her service? Men sometimes wonder that we call her Mother of life, of mercy, of salvation; what are all these titles compared to that one name, Mother of God?

Diff., ii, 3

January 2

Memorial of Saint Basil the Great and Saint Gregory Nazianzen

It often happens that men of very dissimilar talents tastes are attracted together by their very dissimilitude ... Gregory the affectionate, the tender-hearted, the man of quick feelings, the accomplished, the eloquent preacher, – and Basil, the man of firm resolve and hard deeds, the high-minded ruler of Christ's flock, the diligent labourer in the field of ecclesiastical politics. Thus they differed; yet not as if they had not much in common still; both had the blessing and the discomfort of a sensitive mind; both were devoted to an ascetic life; both were men of classical tastes; both were special champions of the Catholic creed; both were skilled in argument, and successful in their use of it; both were in highest place in the Church, the one Exarch of Cæsarea, the other Patriarch of Constantinople.

HS, ii, CF, 3

January 3

The Most Holy Name of Jesus, Optional Memorial

Some sacred place or sacred name is like a magic spell to those whose hearts are accustomed to the thought of religion, or are in any way disposed and prepared by God's grace ... To holy people the very name of Jesus is a name to feed upon, a name to transport ... These are the words which can raise the dead and transfigure and beatify the living.

CS, 3

January 4

> Hid are the saints of God; –
> Uncertified by high angelic sign;
> Nor raiment soft, nor empire's golden rod
> 　Marks them divine.
> Theirs but the unbought air, earth's parent sod,
> 　And the sun's smile benign; –
> Christ rears His throne within the secret heart,
> 　From the haughty world apart.

VV, 'The Hidden Ones'

January 5

We are very apt to wish we had been born in the days of Christ, and in this way we excuse our misconduct, when conscience reproaches us. We say, that had we had the advantage of being with Christ, we should have had stronger motives, stronger restraints against sin. I answer, that so far from our sinful habits being reformed by the presence of Christ, the chance is, that those same habits would have hindered us from recognizing Him. We should not have known He was present; and if He had even told us who He was, we should not have believed Him. Nay, had we seen His miracles (incredible as it may seem), even they would not have made any lasting impression on us.

PS, iv, 16

January 6

Epiphany

The Epiphany is a season especially set apart for adoring the glory of Christ ... In the Epiphany and the weeks after it, we celebrate Him, not as on His field of battle, or in His solitary retreat, but as an august and glorious King; we view Him as the Object of our worship. Then only, during His whole earthly history, did He fulfil the type of Solomon, and held (as I may say) a court, and received the homage of His subjects; viz. when He was an infant. His throne was His undefiled Mother's arms; His chamber of state was a cottage or a cave; the worshippers were the wise men of the East, and they brought presents, gold, frankincense, and myrrh ...

Christ, the true Revealer of secrets, and the Dispenser of the bread of life, the true wisdom and majesty of the Father, manifested His glory but in His early years, and then the Sun of Righteousness was clouded. For He was not to reign really, till He left the world. He has reigned ever since; nay, reigned *in* the world, though He is not in sensible presence in it – the invisible King of a visible kingdom – for He came on earth but to show what His reign would be, after He had left it, and to submit to suffering and dishonour, that He *might* reign.

PS, vii, 6

January 7

Saint Raymond of Peñafort, Patron Saint of Canon Lawyers and Lawyers, Optional Memorial

The kingdom of Christ, though not of this world, yet is in the world, and has a visible, material, social shape. It consists of men, and it has developed according to the laws under which combinations of men develop. It has an external aspect similar to all other kingdoms.

Ess., ii, 12

January 8

It is a sort of degradation of a divine work to consider it under an earthly form; but it is no irreverence, since our Lord Himself, its Author and Guardian, bore one also. Christianity differs from other religions and philosophies, in what is superadded to earth from heaven; not in kind, but in origin; not in its nature, but in its personal characteristics; being informed and quickened by what is more than intellect, by a divine spirit.

Dev., 2

January 9

The Church is a collection of souls, brought together in one by God's secret grace, though that grace comes to them through visible instruments, and unites them to a visible hierarchy. What is seen, is not the whole of the Church, but the visible part of it. When we say that Christ loves His Church, we mean that He loves, nothing of earthly nature, but the fruit of His own grace; – the varied fruits of His grace in innumerable hearts, viewed as brought together in unity of faith and love and obedience, of sacraments, and doctrine, and order, and worship. The object which He contemplates, which He loves in the Church, is not human nature simply, but human nature illuminated and renovated by His own supernatural power

OS, 4

January 10

To consider the world in its length and breadth, its various history, the many races of man, their starts, their fortunes, their mutual alienation, their conflicts; and then their ways, habits, governments, forms of worship; their enterprises, their aimless courses, their random achievements and acquirements, the impotent conclusion of long-standing facts, the tokens so faint and broken of a super-intending design, the blind evolution of what turn out to be great powers or truths, the progress of things, as if from unreasoning elements, not towards final causes, the greatness and littleness of man, his far-reaching aims, his short duration, the curtain hung over his futurity, the disappointments of life, the defeat of good, the success of evil, physical pain, mental anguish, the prevalence and intensity of sin, the pervading idolatries, the corruptions, the dreary hopeless irreligion, that condition of the whole race, so fearfully yet exactly described in the Apostle's words, "having no hope and without God in the world," – all this is a vision to dizzy and appal; and inflicts upon the mind the sense of a profound mystery, which is absolutely beyond human solution.

What shall be said to this heart-piercing, reason-bewildering fact? I can only answer, that either there is no Creator, or this living society of men is in a true sense discarded from His presence.

Apo., 5

January 11

Every event of this world is a type of those that follow, history proceeding forward as a circle ever enlarging.

DA, 2

January 12

A Temple there has been upon earth, a spiritual Temple, made up of living stones, a Temple, as I may say, composed of souls ... Wherever there is faith and love, this Temple is; faith and love, with the Name of Christ, are as heavenly charms and spells, to make present to us this Divine Temple, in every part of Christ's kingdom.

PS, vi, 20

January 13

Saint Hilary of Poitiers, Optional Memorial

What is a mystery in doctrine, but a difficulty or inconsistency in the intellectual expression of it? And what reason is there for supposing, that Revelation addresses itself to the intellect, except so far as intellect is necessary for conveying and fixing its truths on the heart? Why are we not content to take and use what is given us, without asking questions?

Ari., 2.5

January 14

A man who fancies he can find out truth by himself, disdains revelation. He who thinks he *has* found it out, is *impatient* of revelation. He fears it will interfere with his own imaginary discoveries, he is unwilling to consult it; and when it does interfere, then he is angry.

PS, i, 17

January 15

Faith [is] not opposed to reason, but anticipates it. It is a *short* cut.
SN, April 7 1872

January 16

Faith ... does not demand evidence so strong as is necessary for what is commonly considered a rational conviction, or belief on the ground of Reason; and why? For this reason, because it is mainly swayed by antecedent considerations. In this way it is, that the two principles are opposed to one another: Faith is influenced by previous notices, prepossessions, and (in a good sense of the word) prejudices; but Reason, by direct and definite proof. The mind that believes is acted upon by its own hopes, fears, and existing opinions; whereas it is supposed to reason severely, when it rejects antecedent proof of a fact, – rejects every thing but the actual evidence producible in its favour ... When the probabilities we assume do not really exist, or our wishes are inordinate, or our opinions are wrong, our Faith degenerates into weakness, extrava-gance, superstition, enthusiasm, bigotry, prejudice, as the case may be; but when our prepossessions are unexceptionable, then we are right in believing or not believing, not indeed without, but upon slender evidence ...

Faith is a moral principle. It is created in the mind, not so much by facts, as by probabilities; and since probabilities have no definite ascertained value, and are reducible to no scientific standard, what are such to each individual, depends on his moral temperament. A good and a bad man will think very different things probable. In the judgment of a rightly disposed mind, objects are desirable and attainable which irreligious men will consider to be but fancies. Such a correct moral judgment and view of things is the very medium in which the argument for Christianity has its constraining influence; a faint proof under circumstances being more availing than a strong one, apart from those circumstances ...

A man is responsible for his faith, because he is responsible for his likings and dislikings, his hopes and his opinions, on all of which his faith depends.

US, 10

January 17

St Anthony of Egypt, Memorial

Anthony held that faith had power with God for any work: and he took delight in contrasting with this privilege of exercising faith that poor measure of knowledge which is all that sight and reason open on us at the utmost. He seems to have felt there was a divine spirit and power in Christianity such as irresistibly to commend it to religious and honest minds, coming home to the heart with the same conviction which any high moral precept carries with it, and leaving argumentation behind as comparatively useless, except by way of curiously investigating motives and reasons for the satis-faction of the philosophical analyst. And then, when faith was once in operation, it was the instrument of gaining the knowledge of truths which reason could but feebly presage, or could not even have imagined.

HS, ii, CF, 6

January 18

The Gospel has its mysteries, its difficulties, and secret things, which the Holy Spirit does not remove. The grace promised us is given, not that we may know more, but that we may do better ... It enables us to change our fallen nature from evil to good, "to make ourselves a new heart and a new spirit." But it tells us nothing for the *sake* of telling it; neither in His Holy Word, nor through our consciences, has the Blessed Spirit thought fit so to act.

PS, i, 16

January 19

No revelation can be complete and systematic, from the weakness of the human intellect; *so far as* it is not such, it is mysterious. When nothing is revealed, nothing is known, and there is nothing to contemplate or marvel at; but when something is revealed, and only something, for all cannot be, there are forthwith difficulties and perplexities. A Revelation is religious doctrine viewed on its illuminated side; a Mystery is the selfsame doctrine viewed on the side unilluminated. Thus Religious Truth is neither light nor darkness, but both together; it is like the dim view of a country seen in the twilight, with forms half extricated from the darkness, with broken lines, and isolated masses. Revelation, in this way of considering it, is not a revealed *system*, but consists of a number of detached and incomplete truths belonging to a vast system unrevealed, of doctrines and injunctions mysteriously connected together; that is, connected by unknown media, and bearing upon unknown portions of the system.

Ess., i, 2

January 20

Saint Fabian, pope and martyr, or Saint Sebastian, martyr, Optional Memorial

You read ... in the lives of Saints, the wonderful account of their conflicts, and their triumphs over the enemy. They are ... like heroes of romance, so gracefully, so nobly, so royally do they bear themselves. Their actions are as beautiful as fiction, yet as real as fact.

Mix., 5

January 21

Saint Agnes, virgin and martyr, Memorial

The Virginity of the Gospel ... is not a state of independence or isolation, or dreary pride, or barren indolence, or crushed affections; man is made for sympathy, for the interchange of love, for self-denial for the sake of another dearer to him than himself. The Virginity of the Christian soul is a marriage with Christ ...

St Agnes ... when offered for husband a Roman nobleman, answered that she had found a better spouse.

OP, 18

January 22

Saint Vincent, deacon and martyr, Optional Memorial

All of us must rely on something; all must look up to, admire, court, make themselves one with something. Most men cast in their lot with the visible world; but true Christians with Saints and Angels.

PS, iv, 15

January 23

The divinely-enlightened mind sees in Christ the very Object whom it desires to love and worship, – the Object correlative of its own affections; and it trusts Him, or believes, from loving Him.

US, 12

January 24

Saint Francis de Sales, bishop and doctor, Memorial

Cor ad cor loquitur ['Heart speaks to heart']
Newman's motto as a Cardinal, adapting '*cor cordi loquitur*', Saint Francis de Sales

January 25

The Conversion of Saint Paul, apostle, Feast

When Almighty God would convert the world, opening the door of faith to the Gentiles, who was the chosen preacher of His mercy? Not one of Christ's first followers. To show His power, He put forth His hand into the very midst of the persecutors of His Son, and seized upon the most strenuous among them ... Saul, the persecutor, was converted, and preached Christ in the synagogues ...

St. Paul is ... the spiritual father of the Gentiles; and in the history of his sin and its most gracious forgiveness, he exemplifies far more than his brother Apostles his own Gospel; that we are all guilty before God, and can be saved only by His free bounty ...

St. Paul's previous course of life rendered him, perhaps, after his conversion, more fit an instrument of God's purposes towards the Gentiles, as well as a more striking specimen of it ... His awful rashness and blindness, his self-confident, headstrong, cruel rage against the worshippers of the true Messiah, then his strange conversion, then the length of time that elapsed before his solemn ordination, during which he was left to meditate in private on all that had happened, and to anticipate the future, – all this constituted a peculiar preparation for the office of preaching to a lost world, dead in sin. It gave him an extended insight, on the one hand, into the ways and designs of Providence, and, on the other hand, into the workings of sin in the human heart, and the various modes of thinking in which the mind is actually trained. It taught him not to despair of the worst sinners, to be sharp-sighted in detecting the sparks of faith amid corrupt habits of life, and to enter into the various temptations to which human nature is exposed. It wrought in him a profound humility, which disposed him (if we may say so) to bear meekly the abundance of the revelations given him; and it imparted to him a practical wisdom how to apply them to the conversion of others, so as to be weak with the weak, and strong with the strong, to bear their burdens, to instruct and encourage them, to "strengthen his brethren," to rejoice and weep with them; in a word, to be an earthy *Paraclete*, the comforter, help, and guide of his brethren.

PS, ii, 9

January 26

Saints Timothy and Titus, bishops, Memorial

The Apostles ... did not rest their cause on argument; they did not rely on eloquence, wisdom, or reputation; nay, nor did they make miracles necessary to the enforcement of their claims. They did not resolve faith into sight or reason; they contrasted it with both, and bade their hearers believe, sometimes in spite, sometimes in default, sometimes in aid, of sight and reason. They exhorted them to make trial of the Gospel.

Jfc., 9

January 27

Saint Angela Merici, virgin, Optional Memorial

Let us take our present happiness, not as our true rest, but, as what the land of Canaan was to the Israelites, – a type and shadow of it.

PS, vii, 6

January 28

Saint Thomas Aquinas, priest and doctor, Memorial

Poetry is the refuge of those who have not the Catholic Church to flee to and repose upon, for the Church herself is the most sacred and august of poets ... What is the Catholic Church, viewed in her human aspect, but a discipline of the affections and passions? What are her ordinances and practices but the regulated expression of keen, or deep, or turbid feeling, and thus a "cleansing," as Aristotle would word it, of the sick soul? She is the poet of her children; full of music to soothe the sad and control the wayward, – wonderful in story for the imagination of the romantic; rich in symbol and imagery, so that gentle and delicate feelings, which will not bear words, may in silence intimate their presence or commune with themselves. Her very being is poetry; every psalm, every petition, every collect, every versicle, the cross, the mitre, the thurible, is a fulfilment of some dream of childhood, or aspiration of youth. Such poets as are born under her shadow, she takes into her service; she sets them to write hymns, or to compose chants, or to embellish shrines, or to determine ceremonies, or to marshal processions; nay, she can even make schoolmen of them, as she made St. Thomas, till logic becomes poetical.

Ess., ii, 16

January 29

What is the main guide of the soul, given to the whole race of Adam, outside the true fold of Christ as well as within it, given from the first dawn of reason, given to it in spite of that grievous penalty of ignorance, which is one of the chief miseries of our fallen state? It is the light of conscience ... I do not say that its particular injunctions are always clear, or that they are always consistent with each other; but what I am insisting on here is this, that it *commands*, – that it praises, it blames, it promises, it threatens, it implies a future, and it witnesses the unseen. It is more than a man's own self. The man himself has not power over it, or only with extreme difficulty; he did not make it, he cannot destroy it. He may silence it in particular cases or directions, he may distort its enunciations, but he cannot, or it is quite the exception if he can, he cannot emancipate himself from it. He can disobey it, he may refuse to use it; but it remains.

This is Conscience; and, from the nature of the case, its very existence carries on our minds to a Being exterior to ourselves; for else whence did it come? and to a Being superior to ourselves; else whence its strange, troublesome peremptoriness? I say, without going on to the question *what* it says, and whether its particular dictates are always as clear and consistent as they might be, its very existence throws us out of ourselves, and beyond ourselves, to go and seek for Him in the height and depth, whose Voice it is. As the sunshine implies that the sun is in the heavens, though we may see it not, as a knocking at our doors at night implies the presence of one outside in the dark who asks for admittance, so this Word within us, not only instructs us up to a certain point, but necessarily raises our minds to the idea of a Teacher, an unseen Teacher: and in proportion as we listen to that Word, and use it, not only do we learn more from it, not only do its dictates become clearer, and its lessons broader, and its principles more consistent, but its very tone is louder and more authoritative and constraining.

OS, 5

January 30

Conscience ... considered as a moral sense, an intellectual sentiment, is a sense of admiration and disgust, of approbation and blame: but it is something more than a moral sense; it is always, what the sense of the beautiful is only in certain cases; it is always emotional. No wonder then that it always implies what that sense only sometimes implies; that it always involves the recognition of a living object, towards which it is directed. Inanimate things cannot stir our affections; these are correlative with persons. If, as is the case, we feel responsibility, are ashamed, are frightened, at transgressing the voice of conscience, this implies that there is One to whom we are responsible, before whom we are ashamed, whose claims upon us we fear.

GA, 5.1

January 31

Saint John Bosco, priest, Memorial

To understand that we have souls, is to feel our separation from things visible, our independence of them, our distinct existence in ourselves, our individuality, our power of acting for ourselves this way or that way, our accountableness for what we do. These are the great truths which lie wrapped up indeed even in a child's mind, and which God's grace can unfold there in spite of the influence of the external world; but at first this outward world prevails. We look off from self to the things around us, and forget ourselves in them.

PS, i, 2

February

February 1

Establishment of the English Oratory at Maryvale, 1848

What is so powerful an incentive to preaching as the sure belief that it is the preaching of the truth? ... We come among you, because we believe there is but one way of salvation, marked out from the beginning, and that you are not walking along it; we come among you as ministers of that extraordinary grace of God, which you need; we come among you because we have received a great gift from God ourselves, and wish you to be partakers of our joy.

Mix., 1

February 2

Presentation of the Lord, Feast

A little child is brought to the Temple, as all first-born children were brought. There is nothing here uncommon or striking, so far. His parents are with him, poor people, bringing the offering of pigeons or doves, for the purification of the mother. They are met in the Temple by an old man, who takes the child in his arms, offers a thanksgiving to God, and blesses the parents; and next are joined by a woman of a great age, a widow of eighty-four years, who had exceeded the time of useful service, and seemed to be but a fit prey for death. She gives thanks also, and speaks concerning the child to other persons who are present. Then all retire.

Now, there is evidently nothing great or impressive in this; nothing to excite the feelings, or interest the imagination. We know what the world thinks of such a group as I have described. The weak and helpless, whether from age or infancy, it looks upon negligently and passes by. Yet all this that happened was really the solemn fulfilment of an ancient and emphatic prophecy. The infant in arms was the Saviour of the world, the rightful heir, come in disguise of a stranger to visit His own house. The Scripture had said, "The Lord whom ye seek shall suddenly come to His Temple: but who may abide the day of His coming, and who may stand when He appeareth?" He had now taken possession ... "The glory of this latter House shall be greater than of the former," (Haggai ii. 9.) was the announcement made in another prophecy. Behold the glory; a little child and his parents, two aged persons, and a congregation without name or memorial. "The kingdom of God cometh not with observation."

PS, ii, 10

February 3

Saint Blaise, bishop and martyr, or Saint Ansgar, bishop, Optional Memorial

The Christian lives in the past and in the future, and in the unseen; in a word, he lives in no small measure in the unknown. And it is one of his duties, and a part of his work, to make the unknown known; to create within him an image of what is absent, and to realise by faith what he does not see. For this purpose he is granted certain outlines and rudiments of the truth, and from thence he learns to draw it out into its full proportions and its substantial form, – to expand and complete it; whether it be the absolute and perfect truth, or truth under a human dress, or truth in such a shape as is most profitable for him. And the process, by which the word which has been given him, "returns not void," but brings forth and buds and is accomplished and prospers, is Meditation.

LES, 'A Legend of St. Gunleus'

February 4

With Christians, a poetical view of things is a duty – we are bid to colour all things with hues of faith, to see a Divine meaning in every event, and a superhuman tendency. Even our friends around are invested with unearthly brightness – no longer imperfect men, but beings taken into Divine favour, stamped with His seal, and in training for future happiness. It may be added, that the virtues peculiarly Christian are especially poetical – meekness, gentleness, compassion, contentment, modesty, not to mention the devotional virtues.

Ess., i, 1

February 5

Saint Agatha, virgin and martyr, Memorial

All things live in Thee. Whatever there is of being, of life, of excellence, of enjoyment, of happiness, in the whole creation, is, in its substance, simply and absolutely Thine. It is by dipping into the ocean of Thy infinite perfections that all beings have whatever they have of good. All the beautifulness and majesty of the visible world is a shadow or a glimpse of Thee, or the manifestation or operation in a created medium of one or other of Thy attributes.

MD, 3.17

February 6

Saints Paul Miki and companions, martyrs, Memorial

Christians are those who profess to have the love of the truth in their hearts; and when Christ asks them whether they so love Him as to be able to drink of His cup, and partake of His Baptism, they answer, "We are able," and their profession issues in a wonderful fulfilment. They love God and they give up the world.

SD, 19

February 7

The Holy Ghost ... dwells in body and soul, as in a temple ... He pervades us (if it may be so said) as light pervades a building, or as a sweet perfume the folds of some honourable robe; so that, in Scripture language, we are said to be in Him, and He in us. It is plain that such an inhabitation brings the Christian into a state altogether new and marvellous, far above the possession of mere gifts, exalts him inconceivably in the scale of beings, and gives him a place and an office which he had not before. In St. Peter's forcible language, he becomes "partaker of the Divine Nature," and has "power" or authority, as St. John says, "to become the son of God."

PS, ii, 19

February 8

Saint Jerome Emiliani or Saint Josephine Bakhita, virgin, Optional Memorial

Christians are not their own, but bought with a price, and, as being so, are become the servants or rather the slaves of God and His righteousness; and this, upon their being rescued from the state of nature ... Christ set us free from Satan only by making us His servants.

PS, iv, 1

February 9

The glory of the Gospel is, not that it *destroys* the law, but that it makes it *cease* to *be* a bondage; not that it gives us freedom *from* it, but *in* it.

PS, iv, 9

February 10

Saint Scholastica, virgin, Memorial

Matrimony is possession – whole possession – the husband is the wife's and no other's, and the wife is the husband's and none but his. This is to enter into the marriage bond, this is the force of the marriage vow, this is the lesson of the marriage ring. And this it is to be married to Jesus. It is to have Him ours wholly, henceforth, and for ever – it is to be united to Him by an indissoluble tie – it is to be His, while he is ours – it is to partake of that wonderful sacrament which unites Him to His blessed Mother on high.

OP, 18

February 11

Our Lady of Lourdes, Optional Memorial

Mary's holiness ... was such, that if we saw her, and heard her, we should not be able to tell to those who asked us anything about her except simply that she was angelic and heavenly.

Of course her face was most beautiful; but we should not be able to recollect whether it was beautiful or not; we should not recollect any of her features, because it was her beautiful sinless soul, which looked through her eyes, and spoke through her mouth, and was heard in her voice, and compassed her all about; when she was still, or when she walked, whether she smiled, or was sad, her sinless soul, this it was which would draw all those to her who had any grace in them, any remains of grace, any love of holy things.

MD, 1.1.6

February 12

Supposing a man of unholy life were suffered to enter heaven, *he would not be happy there*; so that it would be no mercy to permit him to enter.

PS, i, 1

February 13

If our hearts are by nature set on the world for its own sake, and the world is one day to pass away, what are they to be set on, what to delight in, then? Say, how will the soul feel when, stripped of its present attire, which the world bestows, it stands naked and shuddering before the pure, tranquil, and severe majesty of the Lord its God, its most merciful, yet dishonoured Maker and Saviour? What are to be the pleasures of the soul in another life? Can they be the same as they are here? They cannot; Scripture tells us they cannot; the world passeth away – now what is there left to love and enjoy through a long eternity? What a dark, forlorn, miserable eternity that will be! ... If we would be happy in the world to come, we must make us new hearts.

PS, vii, 2

February 14

Saints Cyril, monk, and Methodius, bishop, Memorial

Civilization is that state to which man's nature points and tends; it is the systematic use, improvement, and combination of those faculties which are his characteristic; and, viewed in its idea, it is the perfection, the happiness of our mortal state. It is the development of art out of nature, and of self-government out of passion, and of certainty out of opinion, and of faith out of reason. It is the due disposition of the various powers of the soul, each in its place, the subordination or subjection of the inferior, and the union of all into one whole. Aims, rules, views, habits, projects; prudence, foresight, observation, inquiry, invention, resource, resolution, perseverance, are its characteristics. Justice, benevolence, expedience, propriety, religion, are its recognized, its motive principles. Supernatural truth is its sovereign law. Such is it in its true idea, synonymous with Christianity; and, not only in idea, but in matter of fact also, is Christianity ever civilization, as far as its influence prevails; but, unhappily, in matter of fact, civilization is not necessarily Christianity.

HS, i, 1.7

February 15

Christ showed His love in deed, not in word, and you will be touched by the thought of His cross far more by bearing it after Him, than by glowing accounts of it.

PS, v, 23

February 16

Love is the parent of faith. We believe in things we see not from love of them: if we did not love, we should not believe. Faith is reliance on the word of another; the word of another is in itself a faint evidence compared with that of sight or reason. It is influential only when we cannot do without it. We cannot do without it when it is our informant about things which we cannot do without. Things we cannot do without, are things which we desire. They who feel they cannot do without the next world, go by faith (not that sight would not be better), but because they have no other means of knowledge to go by.

DA, 3.8

February 17

Seven holy founders of the Servite order, Optional Memorial

Of all passions love is the most unmanageable; nay more, I would not give much for that love which is never extravagant, which always observes the proprieties, and can move about in perfect good taste, under all emergencies ... So it is with devotional feelings. Burning thoughts and words are as open to criticism as they are beyond it. What is abstractedly extravagant, may in particular persons be becoming and beautiful, and only fall under blame when it is found in others who imitate them. When it is formalized into meditations or exercises, it is as repulsive as love-letters in a police report.

Diff, ii, 4

February 18

The great difference, in a practical light, between the object of Christianity and of heathen belief, is this – that glory, science, knowledge, and whatever other fine names we use, never healed a wounded heart, nor changed a sinful one; but the Divine Word is with power. The ideas which Christianity brings before us are in themselves full of influence, and they are attended with a supernatural gift over and above themselves, in order to meet the special exigencies of our nature. Knowledge is not "power," nor is glory "the first and only fair;" but "Grace," or the "Word," by whichever name we call it, has been from the first a quickening, renovating, organizing principle. It has new created the individual, and transferred and knit him into a social body, composed of members each similarly created. It has cleansed man of his moral diseases, raised him to hope and energy, given him to propagate a brotherhood among his fellows, and to found a family or rather a kingdom of saints all over the earth; – it introduced a new force into the world, and the impulse which it gave continues in its original vigour down to this day.

DA, 4.3

February 19

The life of Christ brings together and concentrates truths concerning the chief good and the laws of our being, which wander idle and forlorn over the surface of the moral world, and often appear to diverge from each other. It collects the scattered rays of light, which, in the first days of creation, were poured over the whole face of nature, into certain intelligible centres, in the firmament of the heaven, to rule over the day and over the night, and to divide the light from the darkness.

US, 2

February 20

If Christianity be a social religion, as it certainly is, and if it be based on certain ideas acknowledged as divine, or a creed ... and if these ideas have various aspects, and make distinct impressions on different minds, and issue in consequence in a multiplicity of developments, true, or false, or mixed ... what power will suffice to meet and to do justice to these conflicting conditions, but a supreme authority ruling and reconciling individual judgments by a divine right and a recognized wisdom? ... If Christianity is both social and dogmatic, and intended for all ages, it must humanly speaking have an infallible expounder ... If development must be, then, whereas Revelation is a heavenly gift, He who gave it virtually has not given it, unless He has also secured it from perversion and corruption, in all such development as comes upon it by the necessity of its nature, or, in other words, that that intellectual action through successive generations, which is the organ of development, must, so far forth as it can claim to have been put in charge of the Revelation, be in its determinations infallible.

Dev., 2.2–2.3

February 21

Birth of Newman, 1801

Saint Peter Damian, bishop and doctor of the Church, Optional Memorial

Damiani resolved on resigning his bishopric and retiring back to his beloved cloister ... Gibbon speaks ironically of unwilling monks torn out of their retreats and seated on bishops' thrones, but no one could know but themselves how great a blessing the cloister was, and what a great sacrifice to relinquish it. The ten thousand trivial accidents of the day in a secular life which exert a troublous influence upon the soul, dimming its fair surface with many a spot of dust and damp, these give place to a divine stillness, which, to those who can bear it, is the nearest approach to heaven.

Ess., ii, 13

February 22

Chair of Saint Peter, apostle, Feast

Every exercise of Infallibility is brought out into act by an intense and varied operation of the Reason, both as its ally and as its opponent, and provokes again, when it has done its work, a re-action of Reason against it; and, as in a civil polity the State exists and endures by means of the rivalry and collision, the encroachments and defeats of its constituent parts, so in like manner Catholic Christendom is no simple exhibition of religious absolutism, but presents a continuous picture of Authority and Private Judgment alternately advancing and retreating as the ebb and flow of the tide; – it is a vast assemblage of human beings with wilful intellects and wild passions, brought together into one by the beauty and the Majesty of a Superhuman Power, – into what may be called a large reformatory or training-school, not as if into a hospital or into a prison, not in order to be sent to bed, not to be buried alive, but (if I may change my metaphor) brought together as if into some moral factory, for the melting, refining, and moulding, by an incessant, noisy process, of the raw material of human nature, so excellent, so dangerous, so capable of divine purposes.

St. Paul says in one place that his Apostolical power is given him to edification, and not to destruction. There can be no better account of the Infallibility of the Church. It is a supply for a need, and it does not go beyond that need. Its object is, and its effect also, not to enfeeble the freedom or vigour of human thought in religious speculation, but to resist and control its extravagance ... Infallibility cannot act outside of a definite circle of thought, and it must in all its decisions, or *definitions*, as they are called, profess to be keeping within it. The great truths of the moral law, of natural religion, and of Apostolical faith, are both its boundary and its foundation. It must not go beyond them, and it must ever appeal to them.

Apo., 5

February 23

Saint Polycarp, bishop and martyr, Memorial

Polycarp, the familiar friend of St. John, and a contemporary of Ignatius, suffered in his extreme old age ... Before his sentence, the Proconsul bade him "swear by the fortunes of Cæsar, and have done with Christ" ... "Eighty and six years," he answered, "have I been His servant, and He has never wronged me, but ever has preserved me; and how can I blaspheme my King and my Saviour?" When they would have fastened him to the stake, he said, "Let alone; He who gives me to bear the fire, will give me also to stand firm upon the pyre without your nails."

GA, 10.2

February 24

The Supreme Being is of a certain character, which, expressed in human language, we call ethical. He has the attributes of justice, truth, wisdom, sanctity, benevolence and mercy, as eternal characteristics in His nature, the very Law of His being, identical with Himself; and next, when He became Creator, He implanted this Law, which is Himself, in the intelligence of all His rational creatures. The Divine Law, then, is the rule of ethical truth, the standard of right and wrong, a sovereign, irreversible, absolute authority in the presence of men and Angels ... The rule and measure of duty is not utility, nor expedience, nor the happiness of the greatest number, nor State convenience, nor fitness, order, and the *pulchrum*. Conscience is not a long-sighted selfishness, nor a desire to be consistent with oneself; but it is a messenger from Him, who, both in nature and in grace, speaks to us behind a veil, and teaches and rules us by His representatives. Conscience is the aboriginal Vicar of Christ, a prophet in its informations, a monarch in its peremptoriness, a priest in its blessings and anathemas, and, even though the eternal priesthood throughout the Church could cease to be, in it the sacerdotal principle would remain and would have a sway ... Did the Pope speak against Conscience in the true sense of the word, he would commit a suicidal act. He would be cutting the ground from under his feet. His very mission is to proclaim the moral law, and to protect and strengthen that "Light which enlighteneth every man that cometh into the world." On the law of conscience and its sacredness are founded both his authority in theory and his power in fact ...

All sciences, except the science of Religion, have their certainty in themselves; as far as they are sciences, they consist of necessary conclusions from undeniable premises, or of phenomena manipulated into general truths by an irresistible induction. But the sense of right and wrong, which is the first element in religion, is so delicate, so fitful, so easily puzzled, obscured, perverted, so subtle in its argumentative methods, so impressible by education, so biassed by pride and passion, so unsteady in its course, that, in the struggle for existence amid the various exercises and triumphs of the human intellect, this sense is at once the highest of all teachers, yet the least luminous; and the Church, the Pope, the Hierarchy are, in the Divine purpose, the supply of an urgent demand. Natural Religion, certain as are its grounds and its doctrines as addressed to thoughtful, serious minds, needs, in order that it may speak to mankind with effect and subdue the world, to be sustained and completed by Revelation ...

Though Revelation is so distinct from the teaching of nature and beyond it, yet it is not independent of it, nor without relations towards it, but is its complement, reassertion, issue, embodiment, and interpretation. The Pope, who comes of Revelation, has no jurisdiction over Nature ...

I add one remark. Certainly, if I am obliged to bring religion into after-dinner toasts, (which indeed does not seem quite the thing) I shall drink – to the Pope, if you please, – still, to Conscience first, and to the Pope afterwards.

Diff., ii, 5

February 25

It is the peculiarity of the warfare between the Church and the world, that the world seems ever gaining on the Church, yet the Church is really ever gaining on the world. Its enemies are ever triumphing over it as vanquished, and its members ever despairing; yet it abides.

SD, 6

February 26

A Revelation, that is, a direct message from God to man, itself bears in some degree a miraculous character; inasmuch as it supposes the Deity actually to present Himself before His creatures, and to interpose in the affairs of life in a way above the reach of those settled arrangements of nature, to the existence of which universal experience bears witness. And as a Revelation itself, so again the evidences of a Revelation may all more or less be considered miraculous. Prophecy is an evidence only so far as foreseeing future events is above the known powers of the human mind, or miraculous. In like manner, if the rapid extension of Christianity be urged in favour of its divine origin, it is because such extension, under such circumstances, is supposed to be inconsistent with the known principles and capacity of human nature. And the pure morality of the Gospel, as taught by illiterate fishermen of Galilee, is an evidence, in proportion as the phenomenon disagrees with the conclusions of general experience, which leads us to believe that a high state of mental cultivation is ordinarily requisite for the production of such moral teachers. It might even be said that, strictly speaking, no evidence of a Revelation is conceivable which does not partake of the character of a Miracle; since nothing but a display of power over the existing system of things can attest the immediate presence of Him by whom it was originally established; or, again, because no event which results entirely from the ordinary operation of nature can be the criterion of one that is extraordinary.

Mir., 1.1

February 27

Publication of Tract 90, 1841

Anglicanism claimed to hold, that the Church of England was nothing else than a continuation in this country (as the Church of Rome might be in France or Spain) of that one Church of which in old times Athanasius and Augustine were members. But, if so, the doctrine must be the same; the doctrine of the Old Church must live and speak in Anglican formularies, in the 39 Articles. Did it? Yes, it did; that is what I maintained; it did in substance, in a true sense ... While my purpose was honest, and my grounds of reason satisfactory, I did nevertheless recognize that I was engaged in an *experimentum crucis*. I have no doubt that then I acknowledged to myself that it would be a trial of the Anglican Church, which it had never undergone before.

Apo., 3

February 28

The Christian has a deep, silent, hidden peace, which the world sees not, – like some well in a retired and shady place, difficult of access.

PS, v, 5

March

March 1

God, I know that Thou didst create the whole universe very good; and if this was true of the material world which we see, much more true is it of the world of rational beings. The innumerable stars which fill the firmament, and the very elements out of which the earth is made, all are carried through their courses and their operations in perfect concord; but much higher was the concord which reigned in heaven when the Angels were first created. At that first moment of their existence the main orders of the Angels were in the most excellent harmony, and beautiful to contemplate; and the creation of man was expected next, to continue that harmony in the instance of a different kind of being. Then it was that suddenly was discovered a flaw or a rent in one point of this most delicate and exquisite web – and it extended and unravelled the web, till a third part of it was spoilt; and then again a similar flaw was found in human kind, and it extended over the whole race. This dreadful evil, destroying so large a portion of all God's works, is sin.

My God, such is sin in Thy judgment; what is it in the judgment of the world? A very small evil or none at all. In the judgment of the Creator it is that which has marred His spiritual work; it is a greater evil than though the stars got loose, and ran wild in heaven, and chaos came again

MD, 3.4.4

March 2

What have *we* ventured? I really fear, when we come to examine, it will be found that there is nothing we resolve, nothing we do, nothing we do not do, nothing we avoid, nothing we choose, nothing we give up, nothing we pursue, which we should not resolve, and do, and not do, and avoid, and choose, and give up, and pursue, if Christ had not died, and heaven were not promised us. I really fear that most men called Christians, whatever they may profess, whatever they may think they feel, whatever warmth and illumination and love they may claim as their own, yet would go on almost as they do, neither much better nor much worse, if they believed Christianity to be a fable.

PS, iv, 20

March 3

Deeds of obedience are an intelligible evidence, nay, the sole evidence possible, and, on the whole, a satisfactory evidence of the reality of our faith. I do not say that this or that good work tells anything; but a course of obedience says much.

PS, ii, 14

March 4

Saint Casimir, Optional Memorial

The planting of Christ's Cross in the heart is sharp and trying; but the stately tree rears itself aloft, and has fair branches and rich fruit, and is good to look upon.

PS, iv, 17

March 5

Till we, in a certain sense, detach ourselves from our bodies, our minds will not be in a state to receive divine impressions, and to exert heavenly aspirations. A smooth and easy life, an uninterrupted enjoyment of the goods of Providence, full meals, soft raiment, well-furnished homes, the pleasures of sense, the feeling of security, the consciousness of wealth, – these, and the like, if we are not careful, choke up all the avenues of the soul, through which the light and breath of heaven might come to us. A hard life is, alas! no certain method of becoming spiritually minded, but it is one out of the means by which Almighty God makes us so. We must, at least at seasons, defraud ourselves of nature, if we would not be defrauded of grace.

PS, v, 23

March 6

It is the sight of God, revealed to the eye of faith, that makes us hideous to ourselves, from the contrast which we find ourselves to present to that great God at whom we look ... We are contented with ourselves till we contemplate Him.

OS, 2

March 7

Saints Perpetua and Felicity, martyrs, Memorial

If the merits of the martyrs are to assist us, let us merit that assistance by some portion of their bravery.

SN, October 21, 1860

March 8

Saint John of God, religious, Optional Memorial

Take a mere beggar-woman, lazy, ragged, and filthy, and not over-scrupulous of truth – (I do not say she had arrived at perfection) – but if she is chaste, and sober, and cheerful, and goes to her religious duties (and I am supposing not at all an impossible case), she will, in the eyes of the Church, have a prospect of heaven, which is quite closed and refused to the State's pattern-man, the just, the upright, the generous, the honourable, the conscientious, if he be all this, not from a supernatural power – (I do not determine whether this is likely to be the fact, but I am contrasting views and principles) – not from a supernatural power, but from mere natural virtue.

Diff., i, 8

March 9

Saint Frances of Rome, religious, Optional Memorial

The real love of man *must* depend upon practice, and therefore, must begin by exercising itself on our friends around us, otherwise it will have no existence.

PS, ii, 5

March 10

Prayer … is (if it may be said reverently) *conversing* with God … He who does not pray, does not claim his citizenship with heaven.

PS, iv, 15

March 11

It is only by slow degrees that meditation is able to soften our hard hearts, and that the history of Christ's trials and sorrows really moves us. It is not once thinking of Christ or twice thinking of Christ that will do it. It is by going on quietly and steadily, with the thought of Him in our mind's eye, that by little and little we shall gain something of warmth, light, life, and love. We shall not perceive ourselves changing. It will be like the unfolding of the leaves in spring. You do not see them grow; you cannot, by watching, detect it. But every day, as it passes, has done something for them; and you are able, perhaps, every morning to say that they are more advanced than yesterday. So is it with our souls; not indeed every morning, but at certain periods, we are able to see that we are more alive and religious than we were, though during the interval we were not conscious that we were advancing.

PS, vi, 4

March 12

No one can love God aright without fearing Him ... No one really loves another, who does not feel a certain reverence towards him. When friends transgress this sobriety of affection, they may indeed continue associates for a time, but they have broken the bond of union. It is mutual respect which makes friendship lasting ... We cannot understand Christ's mercies till we understand His power, His glory, His unspeakable holiness, and our demerits; that is, until we first fear Him. Not that fear comes first, and then love; for the most part they will proceed together. Fear is allayed by the love of Him, and our love sobered by our fear of Him.

PS, i, 23

March 13

A man serves with a perfect heart, who serves God in all parts of his duty; and, not here and there, but here and there and every-where; not perfectly indeed as regards the quality of his obedience, but perfectly as regards its extent; not completely, but consistently.

PS, v, 17

March 14

The happiness of the soul consists in the exercise of the affections; not in sensual pleasures, not in activity, not in excitement, not in self esteem, not in the consciousness of power, not in knowledge; in none of these things lies our happiness, but in our affections being elicited, employed, supplied ... God alone is the happiness of our souls ... Created natures cannot open us, or elicit the ten thousand mental senses which belong to us, and through which we really live. None but the presence of our Maker can enter us; for to none besides can the whole heart in all its thoughts and feelings be unlocked and subjected ... The consciousness of a perfect and enduring Presence, and it alone, keeps the heart open ... He who is infinite can alone be its measure; He alone can answer to the mysterious assemblage of feelings and thoughts which it has within it.

PS, v, 22

March 15

The most noble repentance (if a fallen being can be noble in his fall), the most decorous conduct in a conscious sinner, is an *unconditional surrender* of himself to God – not a bargaining about terms, not a scheming (so to call it) to be received back again, but an instant *surrender* of himself in the first instance. Without knowing what will become of him, whether God will spare or not, merely with so much hope in his heart as not utterly to despair of pardon, still not looking merely to *pardon* as an *end*, but rather looking to the claims of the Benefactor whom he has offended, and smitten with shame, and the sense of his ingratitude, he must *surrender himself* to his lawful Sovereign. He is a runaway offender; he must come back, as a very first step, before anything can be determined about him, bad or good; he is a rebel, and must lay down his arms.

PS, iii, 7

March 16

Good works (as they are called) are required, not as if they had any thing of merit in them, not as if they could of themselves turn away God's anger for our sins, or purchase heaven for us, but because they are the means, under God's grace, of strengthening and showing forth that holy principle which God implants in the heart, and without which ... we cannot see Him.

PS, i, 1

March 17

Saint Patrick, bishop, Optional Memorial

The glorious St. Patrick was sent to Ireland, and did a work so great that he could not have a successor in it, the sanctity and learning and zeal and charity which followed on his death being but the result of the one impulse which he gave. I cannot forget how, in no long time, under the fostering breath of the Vicar of Christ, a country of heathen superstitions became the very wonder and asylum of all people, – the wonder by reason of its knowledge, sacred and profane, and the asylum of religion, literature and science, when chased away from the continent by the barbarian invaders. I recollect its hospitality, freely accorded to the pilgrim; its volumes munificently presented to the foreign student; and the prayers, the blessings, the holy rites, the solemn chants, which sanctified the while both giver and receiver.

Idea, 1.1

March 18

Saint Cyril of Jerusalem, bishop and doctor, Optional Memorial

In the preaching of the Apostles and Evangelists in the Book of Acts, the sacred mysteries are revealed to individuals in proportion to their actual religious proficiency ... The ancient Fathers ... considered this caution as the result of the most truly charitable consideration for those whom they addressed, who were likely to be perplexed, not converted, by the sudden exhibition of the whole evangelical scheme ... "Should a catechumen ask thee what the teachers have determined, (says Cyril of Jerusalem) tell nothing to one who is without. For we impart to thee a secret and a promise of the world to come. Keep safe the secret for Him who gives the reward. Listen not to one who asks, 'What harm is there in my knowing also?' Even the sick ask for wine, which, unseasonably

given, brings on delirium; and so there come two ills, the death of
the patient and the disrepute of the physician."

Ari., 1.3

March 19

Saint Joseph, husband of the Blessed Virgin Mary, Solemnity

There is but one saint who typifies to us the next world, and that is
St. Joseph. He is the type of rest, repose, peace. He is the saint and
patron of home, in death as well as in life.

SN, May 8, 1870

March 20

The simplicity of a child's ways and notions, his ready belief of
everything he is told, his artless love, his frank confidence, his
confession of helplessness, his ignorance of evil, his inability to
conceal his thoughts, his contentment, his prompt forgetfulness
of trouble, his admiring without coveting; and, above all, his
reverential spirit, looking at all things about him as wonderful, as
tokens and types of the One Invisible, are all evidence of his being
lately (as it were) a visitant in a higher state of things ... A child
is a pledge of immortality; for he bears upon him in figure those
high and eternal excellences in which the joy of heaven consists,
and which would not be thus shadowed forth by the All-gracious
Creator, were they not one day to be realized.

PS, ii, 6

March 21

Joyful people are loving; joyful people are forgiving; joyful people
are munificent. Joy, if it be Christian joy, the refined joy of the
mortified and persecuted, makes men peaceful, serene, thankful,
gentle, affectionate, sweet-tempered, pleasant, hopeful; it is
graceful, tender, touching, winning.

SD, 19

March 22

God was all-complete, all-blessed in Himself; but it was His will to create a world for His glory. He is Almighty, and might have done all things Himself, but it has been His will to bring about His purposes by the beings He has created. We are all created to His glory – we are created to do His will. I am created to do something or to be something for which no one else is created; I have a place in God's counsels, in God's world, which no one else has; whether I be rich or poor, despised or esteemed by man, God knows me and calls me by my name ... He has not created me for naught. I shall do good, I shall do His work.

MD, 3.1.2

March 23

Saint Turibus of Mogrovejo, bishop, Optional Memorial

Christianity ... has its visible polity, and its universal rule, and its especial prerogatives and powers and lessons, for its disciples. But ... it has confined its revelations to the province of theology, only indirectly touching on other departments of knowledge, so far as theological truth accidentally affects them; and it has shown an equally remarkable care in preventing the introduction of the spirit of caste or race into its constitution or administration. Pure nationalism it abhors; its authoritative documents pointedly ignore the distinction of Jew and Gentile, and warn us that the first often becomes the last; while its subsequent history has illustrated this great principle, by its awful, and absolute, and inscrutable, and irreversible passage from country to country, as its territory and its home.

HS, i, 8

March 24

God is an Individual, Self-dependent, All-perfect, Unchangeable Being; intelligent, living, personal, and present; almighty, all-seeing, all-remembering; between whom and His creatures there is an infinite gulf; who has no origin, who is all-sufficient for Himself; who created and upholds the universe; who will judge every one of us, sooner or later, according to that Law of right and wrong which He has written on our hearts. He is One who is sovereign over, operative amidst, independent of, the appointments which He has made; One in whose hands are all things, who has a purpose in every event, and a standard for every deed ... who has with an adorable, never-ceasing energy implicated Himself in all the history of creation, the constitution of nature, the course of the world, the origin of society, the fortunes of nations, the action of the human mind.

Idea, 1.2

March 25

Annunciation of the Lord

How, and when, did Mary take part, and the initial part, in the world's restoration? It was when the Angel Gabriel came to her to announce to her the great dignity which was to be her portion ... It was God's will that she should undertake *willingly* and with *full understanding* to be the Mother of our Lord, and not to be a mere passive instrument whose maternity would have no merit and no reward. The higher our gifts, the heavier our duties. It was no light lot to be so intimately near to the Redeemer of men, as she experienced afterwards when she suffered with him.

MD, 1.2.4

March 26

His coming up from the heart of the earth was a sign for faith, not for sight; and such is His coming down from heaven as Bread.

PS, vi, 9

March 27

One or two men, of small outward pretensions, but with their hearts in their work, these do great things. These are prepared, not by sudden excitement, or by vague general belief in the truth of their cause, but by deeply impressed, often repeated instruction; and since it stands to reason that it is easier to teach a few than a great number, it is plain such men always will be few. Such as these spread the knowledge of Christ's resurrection over the idolatrous world. Well they answered the teaching of their Lord and Master.

PS, i, 22

March 28

Still is the might of Truth, as it has been:
Lodged in the few, obey'd, and yet unseen.
Rear'd on lone heights, and rare,
His saints their watch-flame bear,
And the mad world sees the wide-circling blaze,
Vain searching whence it streams, and how to quench its rays

VV, 'The Course of Truth'

March 29

The philosopher confesses himself to be imperfect; the Christian feels himself to be sinful and corrupt.

US, 1

March 30

God has graciously willed to bring us to heaven; to practise a heavenly life on earth, certainly, is a thing above earth. It is like trying to execute some high and refined harmony on an insignificant instrument. In attempting it, that instrument would be taxed beyond its powers, and would be sacrificed to great ideas beyond itself. And so, in a certain sense, this life, and our present nature, is sacrificed for heaven and the new creature; that while our outward man perishes, our inward man may be renewed day by day.

SD, 7

March 31

We are risen again, and we know it not. We begin our Catechism by confessing that we are risen, but it takes a long life to apprehend what we confess. We are like people waking from sleep, who cannot collect their thoughts at once, or understand where they are. By little and little the truth breaks upon us. Such are we in the present world; sons of light, gradually waking to a knowledge

of themselves. For this let us meditate, let us pray, let us work, –
gradually to attain to a real apprehension of what we are.

PS, vi, 8

April

April 1

We have lost Christ and we have found Him; we see Him not, yet
we discern Him. We embrace His feet, yet He says, "Touch Me
not." How is this? it is thus: we have lost the sensible and conscious
perception of Him; we cannot look on Him, hear Him, converse
with Him, follow Him from place to place; but we enjoy the
spiritual, immaterial, inward, mental, real sight and possession of
Him; a possession more real and more present than that which the
Apostles had in the days of His flesh, *because* it is spiritual, *because*
it is invisible.

PS, vi, 10

April 2

Saint Francis of Paola, hermit, Optional Memorial

To the monk heaven was next door; he formed no plans, he
had no cares ... He "went forth" in his youth "to his work
and to his labour" until the evening of life; if he lived a day
longer, he did a day's work more; whether he lived many days
or few, he laboured on to the end of them. He had no wish
to see further in advance of his journey than where he was to
make his next stage.

HS, 2.4

April 3

Faith opens upon us Christians the Temple of God wherever
we are; for that Temple is a spiritual one, and so is everywhere
present.

PS, iv, 15

April 4

Saint Isidore, bishop and doctor of the Church, Optional Memorial

Philosophy ... is Reason exercised upon Knowledge; or the Knowledge not merely of things in general, but of things in their relations to one another ... It never views any part of the extended subject-matter of knowledge, without recollecting that it is but a part, or without the associations which spring from this recollection. It makes every thing lead to every thing else; it communicates the image of the whole body to every separate member, till the whole becomes in imagination like a spirit, every where pervading and penetrating its component parts, and giving them their one definite meaning. Just as our bodily organs, when mentioned, recall to mind their function in the body, as the word creation suggests the idea of a Creator, as subjects that of a sovereign, so in the mind of a philosopher, the elements of the physical and moral world, sciences, arts, pursuits, ranks, offices, events, opinions, individualities, are all viewed, not in themselves, but as relative terms, suggesting a multitude of correlatives, and gradually, by successive combinations, converging one and all to their true centre.

US, 14

April 5

Saint Vincent Ferrer, priest, Optional Memorial

To maintain a religious spirit in the midst of engagements and excitements of this world is possible only to a saint; nay, the case is the same though our business be one of a charitable and religious nature.

PS, vii, 5

April 6

When persons are convinced that life is short, that it is unequal to any great purpose, that it does not display adequately, or bring to perfection the true Christian, when they feel that the next life is all in all, and that eternity is the only subject that really can claim or can fill their thoughts, then they are apt to undervalue this life altogether, and to forget its real importance ... Yet it should be recollected that the employments of this world, though not themselves heavenly, are, after all, the way to heaven – though not the fruit, are the seed of immortality – and are valuable, though not in themselves, yet for that to which they lead: but it is difficult to realize this. It is difficult to realize both truths at once, and to connect both truths together; steadily to contemplate the life to come, yet to act in this.

PS, viii, 11

April 7

Saint John Baptist de la Salle, priest, Memorial

Those who are trained carefully according to the precepts of Scripture, gain an elevation, a delicacy, refinement, and sanctity of mind, which is most necessary for judging fairly of the truth of Scripture.

PS, viii, 8

April 8

Christ is risen; He is risen from the dead. We may well cry out, "Alleluia, the Lord Omnipotent reigneth." He has crushed all the power of the enemy under His feet. He has gone upon the lion and the adder. He has stopped the lion's mouth for us His people, and has bruised the serpent's head. There is nothing impossible to us now, if we do but enter into the fulness of our privileges, the wondrous power of our gifts.

PS, iv, 23

April 9

He was "manifested in the flesh; justified in the Spirit; seen of Angels; preached unto the Gentiles; believed on in the world; received up into glory;" yet what was the nature of the manifestation? The Annunciation was secret; the Nativity was secret; the miraculous Fasting in the wilderness was secret; the Resurrection secret; the Ascension not far from secret; the abiding Presence secret. One thing alone was public, and in the eyes of the world,

– His Death; the only event which did not speak of His Divinity, the only event in which He seemed a sign, not of power, but of weakness. He was crucified in weakness, but He was not crucified in secret. His humiliation was proclaimed and manifested all over the earth. When lifted up indeed from the earth, He displayed His power; He drew all men to Him, but not from what was seen, but from what was hidden, from what was not known, from what was matter of faith, from His atoning virtue. As far as seen, He was, in holy Simeon's words, "a Sign which should be spoken against." It is not by reason or by sight that we accept and glory in the sign of the Cross; it is by "laying aside all malice, and all guile, and hypocrisies, and envies, and all evil speakings," and "as newborn babes desiring the sincere milk of the word, that we may grow thereby."

PS, vi, 9

April 10

Six out of His seven last words were words of faith and love. For one instant a horrible dread overwhelmed him, when He seemed to ask why God had forsaken Him. Doubtless "that voice was for our sakes;" as when He made mention of His thirst; and, like the other, was taken from inspired prophecy. Perhaps it was intended to set before us an example of a special trial to which human nature is subject, whatever was the real and inscrutable manner of it in Him, who was all along supported by an inherent Divinity; I mean the trial of sharp agony, hurrying the mind on to vague terrors and strange inexplicable thoughts; and is, therefore, graciously recorded for our benefit, in the history of His death, "who was tempted, in all points, like as we are, yet without sin." (Heb. iv. 15.)

PS, iii, 11

April 11

What mind of man can imagine the love which the Eternal Father bears towards the Only Begotten Son? It has been from everlasting, – and it is infinite; so great is it that divines call the Holy Ghost by the name of that love, as if to express its infinitude and perfection. Yet reflect, O my soul, and bow down before the awful mystery, that, as the Father loves the Son, so doth the Son love thee, if thou art one of His elect; for He says expressly, "As the Father hath loved

Me, I also have loved you. Abide in My love." What mystery in the whole circle of revealed truths is greater than this?

The love which the Son bears to thee, a creature, is like that which the Father bears to the uncreated Son. O wonderful mystery! *This*, then, is the history of what else is so strange: that He should have taken my flesh and died for me. The former mystery anticipates the latter; that latter does but fulfil the former. Did He not love me so inexpressibly, He would not have suffered for me. I understand now why He died for me, because He loved me as a father loves his son – not as a human father merely, but as the Eternal Father the Eternal Son. I see now the meaning of that else inexplicable humiliation: He preferred to regain me rather than to create new worlds.

MD, 3.1.3

April 12

Christ is, as it were, walking among us, and by His hand, or eye, or voice, bidding us follow Him. We do not understand that His call is a thing which takes place now. We think it took place in the Apostles' days; but we do not believe in it, we do not look out for it in our own case. We have not eyes to see the Lord; far different from the beloved Apostle, who knew Christ even when the rest of the disciples knew Him not. When He stood on the shore after His resurrection, and bade them cast the net into the sea, "that disciple whom Jesus loved saith unto Peter, It is the Lord." (John xxi. 7.)

PS, viii, 2

April 13

Saint Martin I, pope and martyr, Optional Memorial

This ... O my soul! is what the sinfulness of sin consists in. It is lifting up my hand against my Infinite Benefactor, against my Almighty Creator, Preserver and Judge – against Him in whom all majesty and glory and beauty and reverence and sanctity centre; against the one only God.

MD, 3.4.2

April 14

He who was Almighty, and All-blessed, and who flooded His own soul with the full glory of the vision of His Divine Nature, would still subject that soul to all the infirmities which naturally belonged to it ... When it pleased Him, He could, and did, deprive it of the light of the presence of God. This was the last and crowning misery that He put upon it ... He said, when His passion began, "My soul is sorrowful even unto death;" and at the last, "My God, why hast Thou forsaken Me?" Thus He was stripped of all things.

My God and Saviour, who wast thus deprived of the light of consolation, whose soul was dark, whose affections were left to thirst without the true object of them, and all this for man, take not from *me* the light of Thy countenance, lest I shrivel from the loss of it and perish in my infirmity.

MD, 3.2.2

April 15

Think of the Cross when you rise and when you lie down, when you go out and when you come in, when you eat and when you walk and when you converse, when you buy and when you sell, when you labour and when you rest, consecrating and sealing all your doings with this one mental action, the thought of the Crucified. Do not talk of it to others; be silent, like the penitent woman, who showed her love in deep subdued acts. She "stood at His feet behind Him weeping, and began to wash His feet with tears, and did wipe them with the hairs of her head, and kissed His feet, and anointed them with the Ointment." And Christ said of her, "Her sins, which are many, are forgiven her, for she loved much; but to whom little is forgiven, the same loveth little." (Luke vii. 38, 47.)

PS, v, 23

April 16

Christianity began by considering Matter as a creature of God, and in itself "very good." It taught that Matter, as well as Spirit, had become corrupt, in the instance of Adam; and it contemplated its recovery. It taught that the Highest had taken a portion of that corrupt mass upon Himself, in order to the sanctification of the whole; that, as a first fruits of His purpose, He had purified from all sin that very portion of it which He took into His Eternal Person, and thereunto had taken it from a Virgin Womb, which He had filled with the abundance of His Spirit. Moreover, it taught that during His earthly sojourn He had been subject to the natural infirmities of man, and had suffered from those ills to which flesh is heir. It taught that the Highest had in that flesh died on the Cross, and that His blood had an expiatory power; moreover, that He had risen again in that flesh, and had carried that flesh with Him into heaven, and that from that flesh, glorified and deified in Him, He never would be divided. As a first consequence of these awful doctrines comes that of the resurrection of the bodies of His Saints, and of their future glorification with Him; next, that of the sanctity of their relics; further, that of the merit of Virginity; and, lastly, that of the prerogatives of Mary, Mother of God.

Dev., 10.1

April 17

Among the wise men of the heathen ... it was usual to speak slightingly and contemptuously of the mortal body; they knew no better. They thought it scarcely a part of their real selves, and fancied they should be in a better condition without it. Nay, they considered it to be the cause of their sinning; as if the soul of man were pure, and the material body were gross, and defiled the soul. *We* have been taught the truth, viz. that sin is a disease of *our minds*, of ourselves; and that the whole of us, not body alone, but soul and body, is naturally corrupt, and that Christ has redeemed and cleansed whatever we are, sinful soul and body.

PS, i, 21

April 18

O dear Lord, because Thou so lovest this human nature which Thou hast created. Thou didst not love us merely as Thy creatures, the work of Thy hands, but as men. Thou lovest all, for Thou hast created all; but Thou lovest man more than all. How is it, Lord, that this should be? What is there in man, above others? *Quid est homo, quod memor es ejus?* yet, *nusquam Angelos apprehendit* – "What is man, that Thou art mindful of him?" ... "nowhere doth he take hold of the angels." Who can sound the depth of Thy counsels and decrees? Thou hast loved man more than Thou hast loved the Angels: and therefore, as Thou didst not take on Thee an angelic nature when Thou didst manifest Thyself for our salvation, so too Thou wouldest not come in any shape or capacity or office which was above the course of ordinary human life – not as a Nazarene, not as a Levitical priest, not as a monk, not as a hermit, but in the fulness and exactness of that human nature which so much Thou lovest. Thou camest not only a perfect man, but as proper man; not formed anew out of earth, not with the spiritual body which Thou now hast, but in that very flesh which had fallen in Adam, and with all our infirmities, all our feelings and sympathies, sin excepted.

MD, 3.7.1

April 19

Charity, we know, is a theological virtue, and the love of man is, properly speaking, included in the love of God. "Every one," says St. John, "that loveth Him that begat, loveth him also who is born of Him." Again, "This commandment we have from God, that he who loveth God, love also his brother." But there is another virtue distinct from charity, though closely connected with it. As Almighty God Himself has the compassion of a father on his children, "for He knoweth our frame, He remembereth that we are dust"; so, after His pattern, we are called upon to cherish the virtue of humanity, as it may be called, a virtue which comes of His supernatural grace, and is cultivated for His sake, though its object is human nature viewed in itself, in its intellect, its affections, and its history.

OS, 8

April 20

St. Paul speaks of Christians ... as having a special power within them, which they gain because they are, and when they become Christians ... "the power that worketh in us" ... He compares it to that divine power in Christ our Saviour, by which, working in due season, He was raised from the dead, so that the bonds of death had no dominion over Him. As seeds have life in them, which seem lifeless, so the Body of Christ had life in itself, when it was dead; and so also, though not in a similar way, we too, sinners as we are, have a spiritual principle in us, if we did but exert it, so great, so wondrous, that all the powers in the visible world, all the conceivable forces and appetites of matter, all the physical miracles which are at this day in process of discovery, almost superseding time and space, dispensing with numbers, and rivalling mind, all these powers of nature are nothing to this gift within us.

PS, v, 24

April 21

Saint Anselm of Canterbury, bishop and doctor of the Church, Optional Memorial

Authority in its most imposing exhibition, grave Bishops, laden with the traditions and rivalries of particular nations or places, have been guided in their decisions by the commanding genius of individuals, sometimes young and of inferior rank. Not that uninspired intellect overruled the super-human gift which was committed to the Council, which would be a self-contradictory assertion, but that in that process of inquiry and deliberation, which ended in an infallible enunciation, individual reason was paramount ... In mediæval times we read of St. Anselm at Bari, as the champion of the Council there held, against the Greeks.

Apo., 5

April 22

An honest, unaffected *desire* of doing right is the test of God's true servant.

PS, v, 16

April 23

Saint George, martyr, Optional Memorial

Catholicism ... was the worship which the English people gained when they emerged out of paganism into gospel light. In the history of their conversion, Christianity and Catholicity are one; they are, as in their own nature, so in that history, convertible terms. It was the Catholic faith which that vigorous young race heard and embraced ... they knew not heresy; and, as time went on, the work did but sink deeper and deeper into their nature, into their social structure and their political institutions; it grew with their growth, and strengthened with their strength, till a sight was seen, – one of the most beautiful which ever has been given to man to see, – what was great in the natural order, made greater by its elevation into the supernatural. The two seemed as if made for each other; that natural temperament and that gift of grace; what was heroic, or generous, or magnanimous in nature, found its corresponding place or office in the divine kingdom ... It did indeed become a peculiar, special people, with a character and genius of its own; I will say a bold thing – in its staidness, sagacity, and simplicity, more like the mind that rules, through all time, the princely line of Roman pontiffs, than perhaps any other Christian people whom the world has seen.

OS, 9.1

April 24

Saint Fidelis of Sigmaringen, priest and martyr

To the end of the longest life you are still a beginner. What Christ asks of you is not sinlessness, but diligence ... You cannot be profitable to Him even with the longest life; you can show faith and love in an hour.

PS, v, 4

April 25

Saint Mark the Evangelist, Feast

St. Mark ... abandoned the cause of the Gospel as soon as danger appeared; afterwards, he proved himself, not merely an ordinary Christian, but a most resolute and exact servant of God, founding and ruling that strictest Church of Alexandria ... The *encouragement* which we derive from these circumstances in St. Mark's history, is, that the feeblest among us may through God's grace become strong. And the *warning* to be drawn from it is, to distrust ourselves; and again, not to despise weak brethren, or to despair of them, but to bear their burdens and help them forward, if so be we may restore them.

PS, ii, 16

April 26

Our duties to God and man are not only duties done to Him, but they are means of enlightening our eyes and making our faith apprehensive. Every act of obedience has a tendency to strengthen our convictions about heaven. Every sacrifice makes us more zealous; every self-denial makes us more devoted.

PS, vi, 8

April 27

Heaven and hell are at war for us and against us, yet we trifle, and let life go on at random.

PS, viii, 5

April 28

Saint Peter Chanel, priest and martyr, or Saint Louis Marie de Montfort, priest, Optional Memorial

Place yourselves at the foot of the Cross, see Mary standing there, looking up and pierced with the sword. Imagine her feelings, make them your own. Let her be your great pattern. Feel what she felt and you will worthily mourn over the death and passion of your and her Saviour. Have her simple faith, and you will believe well. Pray to be filled with the grace given to her.

CS, 7

April 29

Saint Catherine of Siena, virgin and doctor of the Church, Memorial

None can know ... the joys of being holy and pure but the holy. If an Angel were to come down from heaven, even he could not explain them to you; nor could he in turn understand what the pleasures of sin are.

PS, vii, 14

April 30

Saint Pius V, pope, Optional Memorial

After our Lord had declared what all who heard seemed to feel to be a hard doctrine, some in surprise and offence left Him. Our Lord said to the Twelve most tenderly, "Will ye also go away?" St. Peter promptly answered ... "Lord, *to whom* shall we go?" ... If Christ were not to be trusted, there was nothing in the world to be trusted; and this was a conclusion repugnant both to his reason and to his heart. He had within him ideas of greatness and goodness, holiness and eternity, – he had a love of them – he had an instinctive hope and longing after their possession. Nothing could convince him that this unknown good was a dream. Divine life, eternal life was the object which his soul, as far as it had learned to realize and express its wishes, supremely longed for. In Christ he found what he wanted. He says, "Lord, to whom *shall* we go?" implying he must go somewhere. Christ had asked, "Will ye also go *away?*" He only asked about Peter's leaving *Himself*; but in Peter's thought to leave Him was to go somewhere else. He only thought of leaving Him *by* taking another god. That negative state of neither believing nor disbelieving, neither acting this way nor that, which is so much in esteem now, did not occur to his mind as possible. The fervent Apostle ignored the existence of scepticism. With him, his course was at best but a *choice of difficulties* – of difficulties perhaps, but still a choice. He knew of no course without a choice, – choice he must make. Somewhither he must go: whither else? If Christ could deceive him, to whom should he go? Christ's ways might be dark, His words often perplexing, but still he found in Him what he found nowhere else, – amid difficulties, a realization of his inward longings. "Thou hast the words of eternal life."

DA, 3.8

May

May 1

Saint Joseph the Worker, Optional Memorial

Whereas Adam was sentenced to labour as a punishment, Christ has by His coming sanctified it as a means of grace and a sacrifice of thanksgiving, a sacrifice cheerfully to be offered up to the Father in His name.

PS, viii, 11

May 2

Saint Athanasius, bishop and doctor, Memorial
Oratory school opened, 1859

The sanctification, or rather the deification of the nature of man, is one main subject of St. Athanasius's theology. Christ, in rising, raises His Saints with Him to the right hand of power. They become instinct with His life, of one body with His flesh, divine sons, immortal kings, gods. He is in them, because He is in human nature; and He communicates to them that nature, deified by becoming His, that them It may deify. He is in them by the Presence of His Spirit, and in them He is seen.

Dev., 4.2

May 3

Saints Philip and James, Apostles, Feast

When the time came for publishing [the Gospel] to the world at large, while [Christ] gradually initiated the minds [of the first Apostles] into the full graciousness of the New Covenant, as reaching to Gentile as well as Jew, He raised up to Himself, by direct miracle and inspiration, a fresh and independent Witness of it from among His persecutors, [St Paul]; so that from that time the Dispensation had (as it were) a second beginning, and went forward upon a twofold foundation, the teaching, on the one hand, of the Apostles of the Circumcision, and of St. Paul on the other ... Of the School of the Circumcision [were] St. Peter, and still more, St. John; St. James, and we may add, St. Philip. St. James is known to belong to the latter, in his history as Bishop of Jerusalem; and, though little is known of St. Philip, yet what is known of him indicates that he too is to be ranked with St. John ... Take the New Testament, as we have received it. It deserves notice, that ... we cannot divide its contents between the two Schools ... They are inextricably united as regards the documents of faith ... The agreement is in essentials – the nature and office of the Mediator, the gifts which He vouchsafes to us, and the temper of mind and the duties required of a Christian.

PS, ii, 17

May 4

In what way inspiration is compatible with that personal agency on the part of its instruments, which the composition of the Bible evidences, we know not; but if anything is certain, it is this, – that, though the Bible is inspired, and therefore, in one sense, written by God, yet very large portions of it, if not far the greater part of it, are written in as free and unconstrained a manner, and (apparently) with as little apparent consciousness of a supernatural dictation or restraint, on the part of His earthly instruments, as if He had had no share in the work. As God rules the will, yet the will is free, – as He rules the course of the world, yet men conduct it, – so He has inspired the Bible, yet men have written it. Whatever else is true about it, this is true, that we may speak of the history or the mode of its composition, as truly as of that of other books; we may speak of its writers having an object in view, being influenced by circumstances, being anxious, taking pains, purposely omitting or introducing matters, leaving things incomplete, or supplying what others had so left. Though the Bible be inspired, it has all such characteristics as might attach to a book uninspired, – the characteristics of dialect and style, the distinct effects of times and places, youth and age, of moral and intellectual character.

DA, 3.3

May 5

St. Paul's epistles ... I consider to be literature in a real and true sense, as personal, as rich in reflection and emotion, as Demosthenes or Euripides; and, without ceasing to be revelations of objective truth, they are expressions of the subjective notwithstanding. On the other hand, portions of the Gospels, of the book of Genesis, and other passages of the Sacred Volume, are of the nature of Science. Such is the beginning of St. John's Gospel, which we read at the end of Mass. Such is the Creed. I mean, passages such as these are the mere enunciation of eternal things, without (so to say) the medium of any human mind transmitting them to us. The words used have the grandeur, the majesty, the calm, unimpassioned beauty of Science.

Idea, 2.2

May 6

Ideas are in the writer and reader of the revelation, not the inspired text itself ... [It could not] be maintained without extravagance that the letter of the New Testament, or of any assignable number of books, comprises a delineation of all possible forms which a divine message will assume when submitted to a multitude of minds.

Dev., 2.1

May 7

If Christianity is a fact, and impresses an idea of itself on our minds and is a subject-matter of exercises of the reason, that idea will in course of time expand into a multitude of ideas, and aspects of ideas, connected and harmonious with one another, and in themselves determinate and immutable, as is the objective fact itself which is thus represented. It is a characteristic of our minds, that they cannot take an object in, which is submitted to them simply and integrally. We conceive by means of definition or description; whole objects do not create in the intellect whole ideas, but are, to use a mathematical phrase, thrown into series, into a number of statements, strengthening, interpreting, correcting each other, and with more or less exactness approximating, as they accumulate, to a perfect image ... And the more claim an idea has to be considered living, the more various will be its aspects; and the more social and political is its nature, the more complicated and subtle will be its issues, and the longer and more eventful will be its course. And in the number of these special ideas, which from their very depth and richness cannot be fully understood at once ... surely we Christians shall not refuse a foremost place to Christianity.

Dev, 2.1

May 8

Prophets or Doctors are the interpreters of the revelation; they unfold and define its mysteries, they illuminate its documents, they harmonize its contents, they apply its promises. Their teaching is a vast system, not to be comprised in a few sentences, not to be embodied in one code or treatise, but consisting of a certain body of Truth, pervading the Church like an atmosphere, irregular in its shape from its very profusion and exuberance; at times separable only in idea from Episcopal Tradition, yet at times melting away into legend and fable; partly written, partly unwritten, partly the interpretation, partly the supplement of Scripture, partly preserved in intellectual expressions, partly latent in the spirit and temper of Christians; poured to and fro in closets and upon the housetops, in liturgies, in controversial works, in obscure fragments, in sermons, in popular prejudices, in local customs.

VM, i, 10

May 9

Revelation ... considered as a Mystery, it is a doctrine enunciated by inspiration, in human language, as the only possible medium of it, and suitably, according to the capacity of language; a doctrine *lying hid* in language, to be received in that language from the first by every mind, whatever be its separate power of understanding it; entered into more or less by this or that mind, as it may be; and admitting of being apprehended more and more perfectly according to the diligence of this mind and that. It is one and the same, independent and real, of depth unfathomable, and illimitable in its extent.

Ess., i, 2.1

May 10

We are told that God has spoken. Where? In a book? We have tried it and it disappoints; it disappoints us, that most holy and blessed gift, not from fault of its own, but because it is used for a purpose for which it was not given. The Ethiopian's reply, when St. Philip asked him if he understood what he was reading, is the voice of nature: "How can I, unless some man shall guide me?" The Church undertakes that office; she does what none else can do, and this is the secret of her power.

Dev., 2.2

May 11

As God is One, so the impression which He gives us of Himself is one; it is not a thing of parts; it is not a system; nor is it any thing imperfect, and needing a counterpart. It is the vision of an object ... Religious men, according to their measure, have an idea or vision of the Blessed Trinity in Unity, of the Son Incarnate and of His Presence, not as a number of qualities, attributes, and actions, not as the subject of a number of propositions, but as one, and individual, and independent of words, as an impression conveyed through the senses ... Creeds and dogmas live in the one idea which they are designed to express, and which alone is substantive; and are necessary only because the human mind cannot reflect upon that idea, except piecemeal, cannot use it in its oneness and entireness, nor without resolving it into a series of aspects and relations. And in matter of fact these expressions are never equivalent to it; we are able, indeed, to define the creations of our own minds, for they are what we make them and nothing else; but it were as easy to create what is real as to define it; and thus the Catholic dogmas are, after all, but symbols of a Divine fact, which, far from being compassed by those very propositions, would not be exhausted, nor fathomed, by a thousand.

US, 15

May 12

Saints Nereus and Achilleus, martyrs, or Saint Pancras, martyr, Optional Memorial

This has been the real triumph of the Gospel, to raise those beyond themselves and beyond human nature, in whatever rank and condition of life, whose wills mysteriously cooperate with God's grace, who, while God visits them, really fear and really obey God, whatever be the unknown reason why one man obeys Him and another not. It has made men saints, and brought into existence specimens of faith and holiness, which without it are

unknown and impossible ... Saints are creations of the Gospel
and the Church.

PS, iv, 10

May 13

Our Lady of Fatima, Optional Memorial

"A great sign appeared in heaven: A woman clothed with the Sun,
and the Moon under her feet; and on her head a crown of twelve
stars" ... Under the image of the Woman, the Church is signified;
but ... the Holy Apostle would not have spoken of the Church
under this particular image, *unless* there had existed a blessed
Virgin Mary, who was exalted on high, and the object of veneration
to all the faithful ... If it is really the Blessed Virgin whom Scripture
represents as clothed with the sun, crowned with the stars of
heaven, and with the moon as her footstool, what height of glory
may we not attribute to her?

Diff., ii, 3

May 14

Mary comes as a second and holier Eve, having the grace of
indefectibility and the gift of perseverance from the first, and
teaching us how to use God's gifts without abusing them.

SN, May 1, 1851

May 15

Newman made a Cardinal, 1879

I have resisted to the best of my powers the spirit of liberalism in
religion ... the doctrine that there is no positive truth in religion,
but that one creed is as good as another ... It is inconsistent with
any recognition of any religion, as *true*. It teaches that all are to
be tolerated, for all are matters of opinion. Revealed religion is
not a truth, but a sentiment and a taste; not an objective fact, not
miraculous; and it is the right of each individual to make it say just
what strikes his fancy. Devotion is not necessarily founded on faith.
Men may go to Protestant Churches and to Catholic, may get good
from both and belong to neither. They may fraternise together in

spiritual thoughts and feelings, without having any views at all of doctrine in common, or seeing the need of them. Since, then, religion is so personal a peculiarity and so private a possession, we must of necessity ignore it in the intercourse of man with man. If a man puts on a new religion every morning, what is that to you? It is as impertinent to think about a man's religion as about his sources of income or his management of his family. Religion is in no sense the bond of society … Religion … is a private luxury, which a man may have if he will; but which of course he must pay for, and which he must not obtrude upon others, or indulge in to their annoyance … It must be borne in mind, that there is much in the liberalistic theory which is good and true; for example, not to say more, the precepts of justice, truthfulness, sobriety, self-command, benevolence … It is not till we find that this array of principles is intended to supersede, to block out, religion, that we pronounce it to be evil.

AR, 'Biglietto Speech'

May 16

The holier a man is, the less is understood by men of the world.

PS, iv, 16

May 17

Holiness can exist without religion; religion cannot exist without holiness.

PS, iv, 21

May 18

Saint John I, pope and martyr, Optional Memorial

Let us bless and praise God for the present peace of the Church, and the freedom of speech and action which He has vouchsafed to us. There have been times when, to be a Christian, was to be an outcast and a criminal, when to profess the faith of the Saints would have subjected us to bonds and imprisonment. Let us thank God that at present we have nothing to fear, but may serve Him zealously, "no man forbidding" us.

PS, v, 19

May 19

Christ is still on earth. He said expressly that He would come again. The Holy Ghost's coming is so really His coming, that we might as well say that He was not here in the days of His flesh, when He was visibly in this world, as deny that He is here now, when He is here by His Divine Spirit.

PS, iv, 16

May 20

Saint Bernadine of Siena, priest, Optional Memorial

The preacher's object is the spiritual good of his hearers ... Earnestness creates earnestness in others by sympathy; and the more a preacher loses and is lost to himself, the more does he gain his brethren. Nor is it without some logical force also; for what is powerful enough to absorb and possess a preacher has at least a *primâ facie* claim of attention on the part of his hearers ... Preachers should neglect everything whatever besides devotion to their one object, and earnestness in pursuing it, till they in some good measure attain to these requisites. Talent, logic, learning, words, manner, voice, action, all are required for the perfection of a preacher; but "one thing is necessary" – an intense perception and appreciation of the end for which he preaches, and that is, to be the minister of some definite spiritual good to those who hear him ... I do not mean that a preacher must aim at *earnestness*, but that he must aim at his *object*, which is to do some spiritual good to his hearers, and which will at once *make* him earnest.

Idea, 2.6

May 21

Saint Christopher Magallanes and companions, martyrs, Optional Memorial

That religion has nothing to do with political matters ... will not be true till it is true that God does not govern the world, for as God rules in human affairs, so must His servants obey in them.

PS, iii, 15

May 22

Saint Rita of Cascia, Optional Memorial

The thing cannot be named in heaven or earth within the limits of truth and obedience which we cannot do through Christ; the petition cannot be named which may not be accorded to us for His Name's sake.

PS, iv, 23

May 23

Be in earnest, and you will speak of religion where, and when, and how you should; aim at things, and your words will be right without aiming.

PS, v, 3

May 24

Death of Ambrose St John, 1875

There is something in moral truth and goodness, in faith, in firmness, in heavenly-mindedness, in meekness, in courage, in loving-kindness, to which this world's circumstances are quite unequal, for which the longest life is insufficient, which makes the highest opportunities of this world disappointing, which must burst the prison of this world to have its appropriate range. So that when a good man dies, one is led to say, "He has not half showed himself, he has had nothing to exercise him; his days are gone like a shadow, and he is withered like grass."

PS, iv, 14

May 25

Saint Bede the Venerable, priest and doctor, Saint Gregory VII, pope, Saint Mary Magdalene de Pazzi, virgin, Optional Memorial

When [the monk] would employ his mind, he turned to Scripture, the book of books, and there he found a special response to the peculiarities of his vocation; for there supernatural truths stand forth as the trees and flowers of Eden, in a divine disorder, as some awful intricate garden or paradise, which he enjoyed the more because he could not catalogue its wonders. Next he read the Holy Fathers, and there again he recognized a like ungrudging profusion and careless wealth of precept and of consolation. And when he began to compose, still he did so after that mode which nature and revelation had taught him, avoiding curious knowledge, content with incidental ignorance, passing from subject to subject with little regard to system, or care to penetrate beyond his own homestead of thought, – and writing, not with the sharp logic of disputants, or the subtle analysis of philosophers, but with the one aim of reflecting in his pages, as in a faithful mirror, the words and works of the Almighty, as they confronted him, whether in Scripture and the Fathers, or in that "mighty maze" of deeds and events, which men call the world's history, but which to him was a Providential Dispensation.

HS, ii, 4

May 26

Saint Philip Neri, priest, Memorial

Philip, on thee the glowing ray
Of heaven came down upon thy prayer,
To melt thy heart, and burn away
All that of earthly dross was there.

Thy soul became as purest glass,
Through which the Brightness Incarnate
In undimm'd majesty might pass,
Transparent and illuminate.

And so, on Philip when we gaze,
We see the image of his Lord;
The Saint dissolves amid the blaze
Which circles round the Living Word.

VV, 'St. Philip in his God'

May 27

Saint Augustin of Canterbury, bishop, Optional Memorial

I need not tell you ... how suddenly the word of truth came to our ancestors in this island and subdued them to its gentle rule; how the grace of God fell on them, and, without compulsion, as the historian tells us, the multitude became Christian; how, when all was tempestuous, and hopeless, and dark, Christ like a vision of glory came walking to them on the waves of the sea. Then suddenly there was a great calm; a change came over the pagan people in that quarter of the country where the gospel was first preached to them; and from thence the blessed influence went forth, it was poured out over the whole land, till one and all, the Anglo-Saxon people were converted by it. In a hundred years the work was done; the idols, the sacrifices, the mummeries of paganism flitted away and were not, and the pure doctrine and heavenly worship of the Cross were found in their stead. The fair form of Christianity rose up and grew and expanded like a beautiful pageant from north to south; it was majestic, it was solemn, it was bright, it was beautiful and pleasant, it was soothing to the griefs, it was indulgent to the hopes of man; it was at once a teaching and a worship; it had a dogma, a mystery, a ritual of its own; it had an hierarchical form. A brotherhood of holy pastors, with mitre and crosier and uplifted hand, walked forth and blessed and ruled a joyful people. The crucifix headed the procession, and simple monks were there with hearts in prayer, and sweet chants resounded, and the holy Latin tongue was heard, and boys came forth in white, swinging censers, and the fragrant cloud arose, and mass was sung, and the saints were invoked; and day after day, and in the still night, and over the woody hills and in the quiet plains, as constantly as sun and moon and stars go forth in heaven, so regular and solemn was the stately march of blessed services on earth, high festival, and gorgeous procession, and soothing dirge, and passing bell, and the familiar evening call to prayer: till he who recollected the old pagan time, would think it all unreal that he beheld and heard, and would conclude he did but see a vision, so marvellously was heaven let down upon earth, so triumphantly were chased away the fiends of darkness to their prison below.

OS, 9.1

May 28

Religion seems ever expiring, schisms dominant, the light of Truth dim, its adherents scattered. The cause of Christ is ever in its last agony, as though it were but a question of time whether it fails finally this day or another … Well may prophets cry out, "How long will it be, O Lord, to the end of these wonders?" how long will this mystery proceed? how long will this perishing world be sustained by the feeble lights which struggle for existence in its unhealthy atmosphere? God alone knows the day and the hour when that will at length be, which He is ever threatening; meanwhile, thus much of comfort do we gain from what has been hitherto, – not to despond, not to be dismayed, not to be anxious, at the troubles which encompass us. They have ever been; they ever shall be; they are our portion.

VM, i, 14

May 29

If the Church dies, the world's time is run.

SD, 8

May 30

The more we love God, the more we are drawn off from *earth* … The Blessed Virgin's Purity arose from the excess of her love.

SN, October 19, 1856

May 31

Visitation of the Blessed Virgin Mary, Feast

The Angel began the salutation [to Mary]; he said, "Hail, thou that art highly favoured; the Lord is with thee; blessed art thou among women" … Her cousin Elizabeth was the next to greet her with her appropriate title. Though she was filled with the Holy Ghost at the time she spake, yet, far from thinking herself by such a gift equalled to Mary, she was thereby moved to use the lowlier and more reverent language. "She spake out with a loud voice, and said, *Blessed art thou* among women, and blessed is the fruit of thy womb."

PS, ii, 12

June

June 1

Saint Justin Martyr, Memorial

[In] the conflict of Christianity with the old established Paganism ... Christianity ... had that hold of the truth which gave its teaching a gravity, a directness, a consistency, a sternness, and a force, to which its rivals for the most part were strangers ... Dogmatism was in teaching, what confession was in act. Each was the same strong principle of life in a different aspect, distinguishing the faith which was displayed in it from the world's philosophies on the one side, and the world's religions on the other ... "No one," says St. Justin, "has so believed Socrates as to die for the doctrine which he taught." "No one was ever found undergoing death for faith in the sun."

Dev., 8.1

June 2

Saints Marcellinus and Peter, martyrs, Optional Memorial

We are bidden lend and give, asking for nothing again; revenge not ourselves; give our cloak when our coat is taken; offer the left cheek when the right is smitten; suffer without complaint; account persons better than they are; keep from bitter words; pray only when others would be impatient to act; deny ourselves for the sake of others; live contented with what we are; preserve an ignorance of sin and of the world: what is all this, but a character of mind which the world scorns and ridicules even more than it hates? a character which seems to court insult, because it endures it? Is not this what men of the world would say of such a one? "Such a man is unfit for life; he has no eye for any thing; he does not know the difference between good and evil; he is tame and spiritless, he is simple and dull, and a fit prey for the spoiler or defrauder; he is cowardly and narrow-minded, unmanly, feeble, superstitious, and a dreamer" ... Yet such is the character of which Christ gave us the pattern; such was the character of Apostles; such the character which has ever conquered the world.

PS, vii, 8

June 3

Saints Charles Lwanga and companions, martyrs, Memorial

Our duty lies in risking upon Christ's word what we have, for what we have not; and doing so in a noble, generous way, not indeed rashly or lightly, still without knowing accurately what we are doing, not knowing either what we give up, nor again what we shall gain; uncertain about our reward, uncertain about our extent of sacrifice, in all respects leaning, waiting upon Him.

PS, iv, 20

June 4

We love, because it is our nature to love; and it is our nature, because God the Holy Ghost has made it our nature.

PS, iv, 21

June 5

Saint Boniface, bishop and martyr, Memorial

As the physical universe is sustained and carried on in dependence on certain centres of power and laws of operation, so the course of the social and political world, and of that great religious organization called the Catholic Church, is found to proceed for the most part from the presence or action of definite persons, places, events, and institutions, as the visible cause of the whole … The conversion of the heathen is ascribed, after the Apostles, to champions of the truth so few, that we may almost count them, such as Martin, Patrick, Augustine, Boniface.

HS, ii, 4

June 6

Saint Norbert, bishop, Optional Memorial

It frequently happens that repentant sinners become more holy and pleasing to God than those who have never fallen.

SD, 2

June 7

There is no Invisible Church yet formed; it is but a name as yet; a name given to those who are hidden, and known to God only, and as yet but half formed, the unripe and gradually ripening fruit which grows on the stem of the Church Visible.

PS, iii, 17

June 8

It was not till after His resurrection, and especially after His ascension, when the Holy Ghost descended, that the Apostles understood who had been with them. When all was over they knew it, not at the time ... God's Presence is not discerned at the time when it is upon us, but afterwards, when we look back upon what is gone and over.

PS, iv, 17

June 9

Saint Ephrem, deacon and doctor, Optional Memorial

The unseen world through God's secret power and mercy, encroaches upon this world; and the Church that is seen is just that portion of it by which it encroaches; and thus though the visible Churches of the Saints in this world seem rare, and scattered to and fro, like islands in the sea, they are in truth but the tops of the everlasting hills, high and vast and deeply rooted, which a deluge covers.

PS, iv, 11

June 10

The very greatness of our powers makes this life look pitiful; the very pitifulness of this life forces on our thoughts to another; and the prospect of another gives a dignity and value to this life which promises it; and thus this life is at once great and little, and we rightly contemn it while we exalt its importance.

PS, iv, 14

June 11

Saint Barnabas the Apostle, Memorial

St. Barnabas ... "was a good man, full of the Holy Ghost and of faith." This praise of goodness is explained by his very name, Barnabas, "the Son of Consolation," which was given him, as it appears, to mark his character of kindness, gentleness, considerateness, warmth of heart, compassion, and munificence.

PS, ii, 23

June 12

Christ Himself vouchsafes to repeat in each of us in figure and mystery all that He did and suffered in the flesh. He is formed in us, born in us, suffers in us, rises again in us, lives in us; and this not by a succession of events, but all at once: for He comes to us as a Spirit, all dying, all rising again, all living. We are ever receiving our birth, our justification, our renewal, ever dying to sin, ever rising to righteousness. His whole economy in all its parts is ever in us all at once; and this divine presence constitutes the title of each of us to heaven; this is what He will acknowledge and accept at the last day. He will acknowledge Himself, – His image in us.

PS, v, 10

June 13

Saint Anthony of Padua, priest and doctor, Memorial

He loves each of us so much that He has died for each one as fully and absolutely as if there were no one else for Him to die for.

MD, 2.9

June 14

When we are awake, we are conscious we are awake, in a sense in which we cannot fancy we are, when we are asleep. When we have discovered the solution of some difficult problem in science, we have a conviction about it which is distinct from that which accompanies fancied discoveries or guesses. When we realize a truth we have a feeling which they have not, who take words for things. And so, in like manner, if we are allowed to find that real and most sacred Object on which our heart may fix itself, a fulness of peace will follow, which nothing but it can give.

PS, v, 22

June 15

The safeguard of Faith is a right state of heart. This it is that gives it birth; it also disciplines it. This is what protects it from bigotry, credulity, and fanaticism. It is holiness, or dutifulness, or the new creation, or the spiritual mind, however we word it, which is the quickening and illuminating principle of true faith, giving it eyes, hands, and feet. It is Love which forms it out of the rude chaos into an image of Christ.

US, 12

June 16

You ask, what it is you need, besides eyes, in order to see the truths of revelation: I will tell you at once; you need light. Not the keenest eyes can see in the dark. Now, though your mind be the eye, the grace of God is the light; and you will as easily exercise your eyes in this sensible world without the sun, as you will be able to exercise your mind in the spiritual world without a parallel gift from without.

Mix., 9

June 17

In the course of time the whole mind of the world ... was absorbed into the philosophy of the Cross, as the element in which it lived, and the form upon which it was moulded. And how many centuries did this endure, and what vast ruins still remain of its dominion! ... The work went on, and at length a large fabric of divinity was reared, irregular in its structure, and diverse in its style, as beseemed the slow growth of centuries; nay, anomalous in its details, from the peculiarities of individuals, or the interference of strangers, but still, on the whole, the development of an idea, and like itself, and unlike any thing else, its most widely-separated parts having relations with each other, and betokening a common origin ... And this world of thought is the expansion of a few words, uttered, as if casually, by the fishermen of Galilee.

US, 15

June 18

A great idea ... is elicited and expanded by trial, and battles into perfection and supremacy. Nor does it escape the collision of opinion even in its earlier years, nor does it remain truer to itself, and with a better claim to be considered one and the same, though externally protected from vicissitude and change. It is indeed sometimes said that the stream is clearest near the spring. Whatever use may fairly be made of this image, it does not apply to the history of a philosophy or belief, which on the contrary is more equable, and purer, and stronger, when its bed has become deep, and broad, and full. It necessarily rises out of an existing state of things, and for a time savours of the soil. Its vital element needs disengaging from what is foreign and temporary, and is employed in efforts after freedom which become wore vigorous and hopeful as its years increase. Its beginnings are no measure of its capabilities, nor of its scope. At first no one knows what it is, or what it is worth. It remains perhaps for a time quiescent; it tries, as it were, its limbs, and proves the ground under it, and feels its way. From time to time it makes essays which fail, and are in consequence abandoned. It seems in suspense which way to go; it wavers, and at length strikes out in one definite direction. In time it enters upon strange territory; points of controversy alter their bearing; parties rise and around it; dangers and hopes appear in new relations; and old principles reappear under new forms. It changes with them in order to remain the same. In a higher world it is otherwise, but here below to live is to change, and to be perfect is to have changed often.

Dev., 1.1

June 19

Saint Romuald, abbot, Optional Memorial

The highest Christian of all is he ... whose heart is so set on things above, that things below as little excite, agitate, unsettle, distress, and seduce him, as they stop the course of nature, as they stop the sun and moon, or change summer and winter.

PS, viii, 11

June 20

Theology both uses logic and baffles it; and thus logic acts both for the protection and for the perversion of religion. Theology is occupied with supernatural matters, and is ever running into mysteries, which reason can neither explain nor adjust. Its lines of thought come to an abrupt termination, and to pursue them or to complete them is to plunge down the abyss. But logic blunders on, forcing its way, as it can, through thick darkness and ethereal mediums ... I do not mean to say that logic cannot be used to set right its own error, or that in the hands of an able disputant it may not trim the balance of truth ... But such a process is circuitous and elaborate; and is conducted by means of minute subtleties which will give it the appearance of a game of skill in matters too grave and practical to deserve a mere scholastic treatment.

Diff., ii, 4

June 21

Saint Aloysius Gonzaga, religious, Memorial

The holy Apostles would without words know all the truths concerning the high doctrines of theology, which controversialists after them have piously and charitably reduced to formulae, and developed through argument.

Dev., 5.4

June 22

Saint Paulinus of Nola, bishop, or Saints John Fisher and Thomas More, martyrs, Optional Memorial

The Church of Christ ... fights and she suffers, in proportion as she plays her part well; and if she is without suffering, it is because she is slumbering. Her doctrines and precepts never can be palatable to the world; and if the world does not persecute, it is because she does not preach.

PS, v, 20

June 23

Almighty God influences us and works in us, through our minds, not without them or in spite of them; as at the fall we did not become other beings than we had been, but forfeited gifts which had been added to us on our creation, so under the Gospel we do not lose any part of the nature in which we are born, but regain what we have lost. We are what we were, and something more.

US, 14

June 24

Birth of Saint John the Baptist, Solemnity

To expect great effects from our exertions for religious objects is natural indeed, and innocent, but it arises from inexperience of the kind of work we have to do, – to change the heart and will of man. It is a far nobler frame of mind, to labour, not with the hope of seeing the fruit of our labour, but for conscience' sake, as a matter of duty; and again, in faith, trusting good *will* be done, though we see it not.

PS, viii, 9

June 25

This whole world is one vast madhouse, of which the inmates, though shrewd enough in matters of this world, yet in spiritual matters are in one way or another mad.

CS, 6

June 26

We know not what we are, or might be. As the seed has a tree within it, so men have within them Angels.

PS, v, 24

June 27

Saint Cyril of Alexandria, bishop and doctor, Optional Memorial

The Incarnation is the antecedent of the doctrine of Mediation, and the archetype both of the Sacramental principle and of the merits of Saints. From the doctrine of Mediation follow the Atonement, the Mass, the merits of Martyrs and Saints, their invocation and *cultus*. From the Sacramental principle come the Sacraments properly so called; the unity of the Church, and the Holy See as its type and centre; the authority of Councils; the sanctity of rites; the veneration of holy places, shrines, images, vessels, furniture, and vestments. Of the Sacraments, Baptism is developed into Confirmation on the one hand; into Penance, Purgatory, and Indulgences on the other; and the Eucharist into the Real Presence, adoration of the Host, Resurrection of the body, and the virtue of relics. Again, the doctrine of the Sacraments leads to the doctrine of Justification; Justification to that of Original Sin; Original Sin to the merit of Celibacy. Nor do these separate developments stand independent of each other, but by cross relations they are connected, and grow together while they grow from one. The Mass and Real Presence are parts of one; the veneration of Saints and their relics are parts of one; their intercessory power and the Purgatorial State, and again the Mass and that State are correlative; Celibacy is the characteristic mark of Monachism and of the Priesthood. You must accept the whole or reject the whole; attenuation does but enfeeble, and amputation mutilate. It is trifling to receive all but something which is as integral as any other portion; and, on the other hand, it is a solemn thing to accept any part, for, before you know where you are, you may be carried on by a stern logical necessity to accept the whole.

Dev., 2.3

June 28

Saint Irenaeus, bishop and martyr, Memorial

[It is] almost a definition of heresy, that it fastens on some one statement as if the whole truth, to the denial of all others, and as the basis of a new faith; erring rather in what it rejects, than in what it maintains: though, in truth, if the mind deliberately rejects any portion of the doctrine, this is a proof that it does not really hold even that very statement for the sake of which it rejects the others.

US, 15

June 29

Saints Peter and Paul, Apostles, Solemnity

The Apostles appealed to men's hearts, and, according to their hearts, so they answered them. They appealed to their secret belief in a superintending providence, to their hopes and fears thence resulting; and they professed to reveal to them the nature, personality, attributes, will, and works of Him "whom their hearers ignorantly worshipped." They came as commissioned from Him, and declared that mankind was a guilty and outcast race, – that sin was a misery, – that the world was a snare, – that life was a shadow, – that God was everlasting, – that His Law was holy and true, and its sanctions certain and terrible; – that He also was all-merciful, – that He had appointed a Mediator between Him and them, who had removed all obstacles, and was desirous to restore them, and that He had sent themselves to explain how. They said that that Mediator had come and gone; but had left behind Him what was to be His representative till the end of all things, His mystical Body, the Church, in joining which lay the salvation of the world. So they preached, and so they prevailed; using indeed persuasives of every kind as they were given them, but resting at bottom on a principle higher than the senses or the reason. They used many arguments, but as outward forms of something beyond argument ... Thus they spread their nets for disciples, and caught thousands at a cast; thus they roused and inflamed their hearers into enthusiasm, till "the Kingdom of Heaven suffered violence, and the violent took it by force." ... Those who had the seed of God within them ... would find day by day, as love increased, increasing experience that what they had ventured boldly amid conflicting evidence, of sight against sight, and reason against reason, with many things against it, and more things for it, they had ventured well. The examples of meekness, cheerfulness, contentment, silent endurance, private self-denial, fortitude, brotherly love, perseverance in well-doing, which would from time to time meet them in their new kingdom, – the sublimity and harmony of the Church's doctrine, – the touching and subduing beauty of her services and appointments, – their consciousness of her virtue, divinely imparted, upon themselves, in subduing, purifying, changing them, – the bountifulness of her alms-giving, – her power, weak as she was and despised, over the statesmen and philosophers of the world, – her consistent and steady aggression upon it, moving forward in spite of it on all sides at once, like the wheels in the Prophet's vision, and this in contrast with the ephemeral and variable outbreaks of sectarianism, – the unanimity and intimacy existing between her widely-separated branches, – the mutual sympathy and correspondence of men of hostile nations and foreign languages, – the simplicity of her ascetics, the gravity of her Bishops, the awful glory shed around her Martyrs, and the mysterious and recurring traces of mirac-ulous agency here and there, once and again, according as the Spirit willed, – these and the like persuasives acted on them day by day, turning the whisper of their hearts into an habitual conviction, and establishing in the reason what had been begun in the will. And thus has the Church been upheld ever since by an appeal to the People, – to the necessities of human nature, the anxieties of conscience, and the instincts of purity; forcing upon Kings a sufferance or protection which they fain would dispense with, and upon Philosophy a grudging submission and a reserved and limited recognition.

Jfc., 9

June 30

First Martyrs of the Church of Rome, Optional Memorial

Our Lord Jesus Christ is the chief and most glorious of Martyrs, as having "before Pontius Pilate witnessed a good confession" (1 Tim. vi. 13.) but we do not call Him a Martyr, as being much more than a Martyr. True it is, He died for the Truth; but that was not the chief purpose of his death. He died to save us sinners from the wrath of God. He was not only a Martyr; He was an Atoning Sacrifice ... He is the supreme object of our love, gratitude, and reverence. Next to Him we honour the noble army of Martyrs; not indeed comparing them with Him, "who is above all, God blessed for ever," or as if they in suffering had any part in the work of reconciliation, but because they have approached most closely to His pattern of all His servants. They have shed their blood for the Church.

PS, ii, 4

July

July 1

Why is it that we, in the very kingdom of grace, surrounded by Angels, and preceded by Saints, nevertheless can do so little, and instead of mounting with wings like eagles, grovel in the dust, and do but sin, and confess sin, alternately? Is it that the *power* of God is not within us? Is it literally that we are *not able* to perform God's commandments? God forbid! We are able. We have that given us which makes us able. We are not in a state of nature. We have had the gift of grace implanted in us. We have a power within us to do what we are commanded to do. What is it we lack? The power? No; the will. What we lack is the real, simple, earnest, sincere inclination and aim to use what God has given us, and what we have in us. I say, our experience tells us this. It is no matter of mere doctrine, much less a matter of words, but of things; a very practical plain matter.

PS, v, 24

July 2

We cannot expect the system of the universe to come over to us; the inhabitants of heaven, the numberless creations of Angels, the glorious company of the Apostles, the goodly fellowship of the Prophets, the noble army of Martyrs, the holy Church universal, the Will and Attributes of God, these are fixed. We must go over to them.

PS, vii, 2

July 3

Saint Thomas the Apostle, Feast

Divine truth [is not] ours to summon at will. If we *determine* that we will find it out, we shall find nothing ... Let us *believe*; evidence will come after faith as its reward, better than before it as its groundwork.

PS, vi, 23

July 4

Saint Elizabeth of Portugal

The Word of Life is offered to a man; and, on its being offered, he has Faith in it. Why? On these two grounds, – the word of its human messenger, and the likelihood of the message. And why does he feel the message to be probable? Because he has a love for it, his love being strong, though the testimony is weak. He has a keen sense of the intrinsic excellence of the message, of its desirableness, of its likeness to what it seems to him Divine Goodness would vouchsafe did He vouchsafe any, of the need of a Revelation, and its probability. Thus Faith is the reasoning of a religious mind, or of what Scripture calls a right or renewed heart, which acts upon presumptions rather than evidence, which speculates and ventures on the future when it cannot make sure of it.

US, 11

July 5

Saint Anthony Zaccaria, priest, Optional Memorial

There are, to be sure, many cogent arguments to lead one to join the Catholic Church, but they do not force the will. We may know them, and not be moved to act upon them. We may be convinced without being persuaded. The two things are quite distinct from each other, seeing you ought to believe, and believing; reason, if left to itself, will bring you to the conclusion that you have sufficient grounds for believing, but belief is the gift of grace.

Mix., 10

July 6

Saint Maria Goretti, virgin and martyr, Memorial

God tells us He ... is compassionate, and full of tender mercy. Yet we do not well know what this means, for how can God rejoice or grieve? By the very perfection of His nature Almighty God cannot show sympathy, at least to the comprehension of beings of such limited minds as ours ... We cannot see God's sympathy; and the Son of God, though feeling for us as great compassion as his Father, did not show it to us while He remained in His Father's bosom. But when He took flesh and appeared on earth, He showed us the Godhead in a new manifestation. He invested Himself with a new set of attributes, those of our flesh, taking into him a human soul and body, in order that thoughts, feelings, affections might be His, which could respond to ours and certify to us His tender mercy. When, then, our Saviour weeps from sympathy ... it is the love of God, the bowels of compassion of the Almighty and Eternal, condescending to show it as we are capable of receiving it, in the form of human nature.

PS, iii, 10

July 7

To believe is to look beyond this world to God, and to obey is to look beyond this world to God; to believe is of the heart, and to obey is of the heart; to believe is not a solitary act, but a consistent habit of trust; and to obey is not a solitary act, but a consistent habit of doing our duty in all things. I do not say that faith and obedience do not stand for separate ideas in our minds, but they stand for nothing more; they are not divided one from the other in fact. They are but one thing viewed differently.

PS, iii, 6

July 8

Our Saviour's words are not of a nature to be heard once and no more, but that to understand them we must feed upon them, and live in them, as if by little and little growing into their meaning.

PS, iii, 10

July 9

Saint Augustine Zhao Rong and companions, martyrs, Memorial

In the Old Covenant, Almighty God first of all spoke the Ten

Commandments from Mount Sinai, and afterwards wrote them. So our Lord first spoke His own Gospel, both of promise and of precept, on the Mount, and His Evangelists have recorded it. Further, when He delivered it, He spoke by way of parallel to the Ten Commandments. And His style, moreover, corresponds to the authority which He assumes. It is of that solemn, measured, and severe character, which bears on the face of it tokens of its belonging to One who spake as none other man could speak. The Beatitudes, with which His Sermon opens, are an instance of this incommunicable style, which befitted, as far as human words could befit, God Incarnate.

Nor is this style peculiar to the Sermon on the Mount. All through the Gospels it is discernible, distinct from any other part of Scripture, showing itself in solemn declarations, canons, sentences, or sayings, such as legislators propound, and scribes and lawyers comment on. Surely everything our Saviour did and said is characterized by mingled simplicity and mystery. His emblematical actions, His typical miracles, His parables, His replies, His censures, all are evidences of a legislature in germ, afterwards to be developed, a code of divine truth which was ever to be before men's eyes, to be the subject of investigation and interpretation, and the guide in controversy. "Verily, verily I say unto you," – "But, I say unto you," – are the tokens of a supreme Teacher and Prophet.

VM, i, 12

July 10

Every word of Christ is good ... All His sacred speeches, though clothed in a temporary garb, and serving an immediate end, and difficult, in consequence, to disengage from what is temporary in them and immediate, yet all have their force in every age, abiding in the Church on earth, "enduring for ever in heaven," and running on into eternity. They are our rule, "holy, just, and good," "the lantern of our feet and the light of our paths," in this very day as fully and as intimately as when they were first pronounced.

PS, iii, 22

July 11

Saint Benedict, abbot, Memorial

St. Benedict ... was the "Father of many nations." He has been styled "the Patriarch of the West." ... [He] found the world, physical and social, in ruins, and his mission was to restore it in the way, not of science, but of nature, not as if setting about to do it, not professing to do it by any set time or by any rare specific or by any series of strokes, but so quietly, patiently, gradually, that often, till the work was done, it was not known to be doing. It was a restoration, rather than a visitation, correction, or conversion. The new world which he helped to create was a growth rather than a structure. Silent men were observed about the country, or discovered in the forest, digging, clearing, and building; and other silent men, not seen, were sitting in the cold cloister, tiring their eyes, and keeping their attention on the stretch, while they painfully deciphered and copied and re-copied the manuscripts which they had saved. There was no one that "contended, or cried out," or drew attention to what was going on; but by degrees the woody swamp became a hermitage, a religious house, a farm, an abbey, a village, a seminary, a school of learning, and a city. Roads and bridges connected it with other abbeys and cities, which had similarly grown up; and what the haughty Alaric or fierce Attila had broken to pieces, these patient meditative men had brought together and made to live again.

HS, ii, 4

July 12

This is the legitimate use of this world, to make us seek for another.

PS, v, 3

July 13

Saint Henry, Optional Memorial

Those who are set on their own ease, most certainly are bad comforters of others; thus the rich man, who fared sumptuously every day, let Lazarus lie at his gate, and left him to be "comforted" after this life by Angels. As to comfort the poor and afflicted is the way to heaven, so to have affliction ourselves is the way to comfort them.

PS, v, 21

July 14

Saint Camillus de Lellis, priest, Optional Memorial

A voluntary or gratuitous mortification in one shape or another, voluntary chastity, voluntary poverty, voluntary obedience, vows of perfection, all this is the very point of contest between the world and the Church, the world hating it, and the Church counselling it.

Mix., 15

July 15

Saint Bonaventure, bishop and doctor, Memorial

Love is the gentle, tranquil, satisfied acquiescence and adherence of the soul in the contemplation of God; not only a preference of God before all things, but a delight in Him because He is God, and because His commandments are good; not any violent emotion or transport, but as St. Paul describes it, long-suffering, kind, modest, unassuming, innocent, simple, orderly, disinterested, meek, pure-hearted, sweet-tempered, patient, enduring.

PS, iv, 21

July 16

Our Lady of Mount Carmel, Optional Memorial

Mary is the most beautiful flower that ever was seen in the spiritual world. It is by the power of God's grace that from this barren and desolate earth there have ever sprung up at all flowers of holiness and glory. And Mary is the Queen of them.

MD, 1.4.3

July 17

It is in proportion as we search our hearts and understand our own nature, that we understand what is meant by an Infinite

Governor and Judge; in proportion as we comprehend the nature of disobedience and our actual sinfulness, that we feel what is the blessing of the removal of sin, redemption, pardon, sanctification, which otherwise are mere words. God speaks to us primarily in our hearts. Self-knowledge is the key to the precepts and doctrines of Scripture. The very utmost any outward notices of religion can do, is to startle us and make us turn inward and search our hearts; and then, when we have experienced what it is to read ourselves, we shall profit by the doctrines of the Church and the Bible.

PS, i, 4

July 18

Many a man seems to have no grasp at all of doctrinal truth. He cannot get himself to think it of importance what a man believes, and what not ... Why? Because the next world is not a reality to him; it only exists in his mind in the form of certain conclusions from certain reasonings. It is but an inference; and never can be more, never can be present to his mind, until he acts, instead of arguing. Let him but act as if the next world were before him; let him but give himself to such devotional exercises as we ought to observe in the presence of an Almighty, All-holy, and All-merciful God, and it will be a rare case indeed if his difficulties do not vanish.

PS, iv, 15

July 19

A bad man, if brought to heaven, would not know He was in heaven ... He would see nothing wonderful there.

PS, iv, 16

July 20

Saint Apollinaris, Optional Memorial

If we only go so far as to realize what Christianity is, when considered merely as a creed, and what stupendous over-powering facts are involved in the doctrine of a Divine Incarnation, we shall feel that no miracle can be great after it, nothing strange or marvellous, nothing beyond expectation.

Mir., 2.4

July 21

Saint Lawrence of Brindisi, Optional Memorial

They who are living religiously, have from time to time truths they did not know before, or had no need to consider, brought before them forcibly; truths which involve duties, which are in fact precepts, and claim obedience. In this and such-like ways Christ calls us now. There is nothing miraculous or extraordinary in His dealings with us. He works through our natural faculties and circumstances of life. Still what happens to us in providence is in all essential respects what His voice was to those whom He addressed when on earth: whether He commands by a visible presence, or by a voice, or by our consciences, it matters not, so that we feel it to be a command.

PS, viii, 2

July 22

Saint Mary Magdalene, Memorial

Our Lord says to St. Mary Magdalen – "Touch Me not, for I am not yet ascended to My Father" (John xx. 17.) [and] here the question arises ... *Why* might not our Lord be touched *before* His ascension, and how *could* He be touched *after* it? But Christ speaks, it would seem, thus ... "Hitherto you have only known Me after the flesh. I have lived among you as a man. You have been permitted to approach Me sensibly, to kiss and embrace My feet, to pour ointment upon My head. But all this is at an end, now that I have died and risen again in the power of the Spirit. A glorified state of existence is begun in Me, and will soon be perfected ... When I am ascended, then the change will be completed. To pass hence to the Father in My bodily presence, is to descend from the Father to you in spirit. When I am thus changed, when I am thus present to you, more really present than now though invisibly, then you may touch Me, – may touch Me, more really though invisibly, by faith, in reverence, through such outward approaches as I shall assign. Now you but see Me from time to time; when you see most of Me I am at best but 'going in and out among you.' Thou hast seen Me, Mary, but couldst not hold Me; thou hast approached Me, but only to embrace My feet, or to be touched by My hand; and thou sayest, 'O that I knew where I might find Him, that I might come even to His seat! O that I might hold Him and not let Him go!' Henceforth this shall be; when I am ascended, thou shalt see nothing, thou shalt have everything. Thou shalt 'sit down under My shadow with great delight, and My fruit shall be sweet to thy taste.' Thou shalt have Me whole and entire. I will be near thee, I will be in thee; I will come into thy heart a whole Saviour, a whole Christ, – in all My fulness as God and man, – in the awful virtue of that Body and Blood, which has been taken into the Divine Person of the Word, and is indivisible from it, and has atoned for the sins of the world, – not by external contact, not by partial possession, not by momentary approaches, not by a barren manifestation, but inward in presence, and intimate in fruition, a principle of life and a seed of immortality, that thou mayest 'bring forth fruit unto God.'"

Jfc., 9

July 23

Saint Birgitta, religious, Optional Memorial

The presence of Christ, now that it is invisible, brings with it a host of high and mysterious feelings, such as nothing else can inspire. The thought of our Saviour, absent yet present, is like that of a friend taken from us, but, as it were, in dream returned to us, though in this case not in dream, but in reality and truth.

PS, v, 2

July 24

Saint Sharbel Makhluf, hermit, Optional Memorial

"I have more understanding than the aged, *because* I keep Thy commandments." By obeying the commands of Scripture, we learn that these commands really come from God; by trying we make proof; by doing we come to know.

PS, viii, 8

July 25

Saint James, Apostle, Feast

Justifying faith ... is not (as it were) a shadow or phantom, which flits about without voice or power, but it is faith developed into height and depth and breadth, as if in a bodily form, not as a picture but as an image, with a right side and a left, a without and a within; not a mere impression or sudden gleam of light upon the soul, not knowledge, or emotion, or conviction, which ends with itself, but the beginning of that which is eternal, the operation of the Indwelling Power which acts from within us outwards and round about us, works in us mightily, so intimately with our will as to be in a true sense one with it; pours itself out into our whole mind, runs over into our thoughts, desires, feelings, purposes, attempts, and works, combines them all together into one, makes the whole man its one instrument, and justifies him into one holy and gracious ministry, one embodied lifelong act of faith, one "sacrifice, holy, acceptable to God, which is his reasonable service." Such is faith, springing up out of the immortal seed of love, and ever budding forth in new blossoms and maturing new fruit, existing indeed in feelings but passing on into acts ... Whereas Faith on our part fitly corresponds, or is the correlative, as it is called, to grace on God's part, Sacraments are but the manifestation of grace, and good works are but the manifestation of faith; so that, whether we say we are justified by faith, or by works or by Sacraments, all these but mean this one doctrine, that we are justified by grace, which is given through Sacraments, impetrated by faith, manifested in works.

Jfc., 10

July 26

Saints Joachim and Anne, Memorial

Christ has purchased for us what we lost in Adam, our garment of innocence. He has bid us and enabled us to become as little children; He has purchased for us the grace of *simplicity*, which, though one of the highest, is very little thought about, is very little sought after. We have, indeed, a general idea what love is, and hope, and faith, and truth, and purity, though a poor idea; but we are almost blind to what is one of the first elements of Christian perfection, that simple-mindedness which springs from the heart's being *whole* with God, entire, undivided.

PS, viii, 18

July 27

Love is the material (so to speak) out of which all graces are made, the quality of mind which is the fruit of regeneration, and in which the Spirit dwells ... "Charity," or love, "never faileth." Faith and hope are graces of an imperfect state, and they cease with that state; but love is greater, because it is perfection. Faith and hope are graces, as far as we belong to this world, – which is for a time; but love is a grace, because we are creatures of God whether here or elsewhere, and partakers in a redemption which is to last for ever. Faith will not be when there is sight, nor hope when there is enjoyment; but love will (as we believe) increase more and more to all eternity. Faith and hope are means by which we express our love: we believe God's word, because we love it; we hope after heaven, because we love it. We should not have any hope or concern about it, unless we loved it; we should not trust or confide in the God of heaven, unless we loved Him. Faith, then, and hope are but instruments or expressions of love; but as to love itself, we do not love because we believe, for the devils believe, yet do not love; nor do we love because we hope, for hypocrites hope, who do not love. But we love for no cause beyond itself.

PS, iv, 21

July 28

Were it not for faith, love would become impatient.

PS, v, 6

July 29

Saint Martha, Memorial

Wherever faith in Christ is, there is Christ Himself. He said to Martha, "Believest thou this?" Wherever there is a heart to answer, "Lord, I believe," there Christ is present. There our Lord vouchsafes to stand, though unseen – whether over the bed of death or over the grave; whether we ourselves are sinking or those who are dear to us. Blessed be his name! nothing can rob us of this consolation: we will be as certain, through His grace, that He is standing over us in love, as though we saw Him.

PS, iii, 10

July 30

Saint Peter Chrysologus, bishop and doctor, Optional Memorial

It is not an easy thing to learn that new language which Christ has brought us. He has interpreted all things for us in a new way; He has brought us a religion which sheds a new light on all that happens. Try to learn this language. Do not get it by rote, or speak it as a thing of course. Try to understand what you say. Time is short, eternity is long; God is great, man is weak; he stands between heaven and hell; Christ is his Saviour; Christ has suffered for him. The Holy Ghost sanctifies him; repentance purifies him, faith justifies, works save. These are solemn truths, which need not be actually spoken, except in the way of creed or of teaching; but which must be laid up in the heart. That a thing is true, is no reason that it should be said, but that it should be done; that it should be acted upon; that it should be made our own inwardly.

PS, v, 3

July 31

Saint Ignatius of Loyola, priest, Memorial

The palm of religious Prudence, in the Aristotelic sense of that comprehensive word, belongs to the School of Religion of which St. Ignatius is the Founder. That great Society is ... the school and pattern of discretion, practical sense, and wise government. Sublimer conceptions or more profound speculations may have been created or elaborated elsewhere; but, whether we consider the illustrious Body in its own constitution, or in its rules for instruction and direction, we see that it is its very genius to prefer this most excellent prudence to every other gift, and to think little both of poetry and of science, unless they happen to be useful.

HS, ii, 4

August

August 1

Saint Alphonsus Maria de Liguori, bishop and doctor, Memorial

It never surprises me to read anything extraordinary in the devotions of a saint. Such men are on a level very different from our own, and we cannot understand them … But we may refrain from judging, without proceeding to imitate … They are beyond us, and we must use them as patterns, not as copies.

Diff., ii, 5

August 2

Saint Eusebius of Vercelli, bishop, or Saint Peter Julian Eymard, priest, Optional Memorial

To know Christ is … to discern the Father of all, as manifested through His Only-begotten Son Incarnate … And thus the Gospels, which contain the memorials of this wonderful grace, are our principal treasures. They may be called the text of the Revelation; and the Epistles, especially St. Paul's, are as comments upon it, unfolding and illustrating it in its various parts, raising history into doctrine, ordinances into sacraments, detached words or actions into principles, and thus everywhere dutifully preaching His Person, work, and will … He is the chief Prophet of the Church, and His Apostles do but explain His words and actions; according to His own account of the guidance promised to them, that it should "glorify" Him. The like service is ministered to Him by the Creeds and doctrinal expositions of the early Church, which we retain in our Services. They speak of no ideal being, such as the imagination alone contemplates, but of the very Son of God, whose life is recorded in the Gospels. Thus every part of the Dispensation tends to the manifestation of Him who is its centre.

PS, ii, 14

August 3

[The] Redeemer … left His Father's courts, He was manifested, He spake; and His voice went out into all lands … Henceforth He is the one principle of life in all His servants, who are but His organs ... He is the sole self-existing principle in the Christian Church, and everything else is but a portion or declaration of Him. Not that now, as then, we may not speak of prophets, and rulers, and priests, and sacrifices, and altars, and saints, and that in a far higher and more spiritual sense than before, but that they are not any of them such of themselves; it is not they, but the grace of God that is in them. There is under the Gospel but One proper Priest, Prophet, and King, Altar, Sacrifice, and House of God. Unity is its characteristic sacrament; all grace flows from One Head, and all life circulates in the members of One Body.

Jfc., 8

August 4

Saint Jean Vianney, priest, Memorial

He took bread, and blessed, and made it His Body; He took wine, and gave thanks, and made it His Blood; and He gave His priests the power to do what He had done. Henceforth, He is in the hands of sinners once more. Frail, ignorant, sinful man, by the sacerdotal power given to him, compels the presence of the Highest.

OS, 6

August 5

Dedication of the Basilica di Santa Maria Maggiore, Optional Memorial

If ... a man does not seek Him where He is, there is no profit in seeking Him where He is not. What is the good of sitting at home seeking Him, when His Presence is in the holy Eucharist?

PS, vii, 11

August 6

Transfiguration of the Lord, Feast

When our Lord was transfigured, He showed us what Heaven is.

PS, vii, 14

August 7

Saint Sixtus II, pope, and companions, martyrs, or Saint Cajetan, priest, Optional Memorial

Christians ... are in Heaven, in the world of spirits, and are placed in the way of all manner of invisible influences. "Their conversation is in heaven;" they live among Angels, and are within reach (as I may say) of the Saints departed. They are ministers round the throne of their reconciled Father, "kings and priests unto God," having their robes washed in the Lamb's blood, and being consecrated as temples of the Holy Ghost.

PS, iii, 18

August 8

Saint Dominic, priest, Memorial

It was the magnificent aim of the children of St. Dominic to form the whole matter of human knowledge into one harmonious system, to secure the alliance between religion and philosophy, and to train men to the use of the gifts of nature in the sunlight of divine grace and revealed truth. It required the dissolution and reconstruction of society to give an opportunity for so great a thought; and accordingly, the Order of Preachers flourished after the old Empire had passed away, and the chaos which followed on it had resulted in the creation of a new world.

OS, 12.2

August 9

Saint Teresa Benedicta of the Cross (Edith Stein), virgin and martyr, Optional Memorial

The Jews are one of the few Oriental nations who are known in history as a people of progress, and their line of progress is the development of religious truth. In that their own line they stand by themselves among all the populations, not only of the East, but of the West. Their country may be called the classical home of the religious principle, as Greece is the home of intellectual power, and Rome that of political and practical wisdom. Theism is their life; it is emphatically their natural religion, for they never were without it, and were made a people by means of it. This is a phenomenon singular and solitary in history, and must have a meaning. If there be a God and Providence, it must come from Him, whether immediately or indirectly.

GA, 10.2

August 10

Saint Lawrence, deacon and martyr, Feast

St. Laurence ... submitted to be burned rather than deliver up the goods with which he had been intrusted for the sake of the poor.

HS, i, 4.1

August 11

Saint Clare, virgin, Memorial
Death of Newman, 1890

[Angel to the soul of Gerontius]
Nor touch, nor taste, nor hearing hast thou now;
Thou livest in a world of signs and types,
The presentations of most holy truths,
Living and strong, which now encompass thee.
A disembodied soul, thou hast by right
No converse with aught else beside thyself;
But, lest so stern a solitude should load
And break thy being, in mercy are vouchsafed
Some lower measures of perception,
Which seem to thee, as though through channels brought
Through ear, or nerves, or palate, which are gone.
And thou art wrapp'd and swathed around in dreams,
Dreams that are true, yet enigmatical;
For the belongings of thy present state,
Save through such symbols, come not home to Thee.

VV, 'Dream of Gerontius'

August 12

Saint Jane Frances de Chantal, religious, Optional Memorial

It is certain that man is not sufficient for his own happiness, that he is not himself, is not at home with himself, without the presence within him of the grace of Him who, knowing it, has offered that grace to all freely. When he was created, then his Maker breathed into him the supernatural life of the Holy Spirit, which is his true happiness; when he fell, he forfeited the divine gift, and with it his happiness also. Ever since he has been unhappy; ever since he has felt a void in his breast, and does not know how to satisfy it. He scarcely apprehends his own need; only the unstudied, involuntary movement of his mind and heart show that he feels it, for he is either languid, dull, or apathetic under this hunger, or he is feverish and restless, seeking first in one thing, then in another, that blessing which he has lost.

OS, 4

August 13

Saints Pontian, pope, and Hippolytus, priest, martyrs, Optional Memorial

What is prayer but the expression, the voice, of faith? ... What ... is faith, but the looking to God and thinking of Him continually, holding habitual fellowship with Him, that is, speaking to Him in our hearts all through the day, praying without ceasing?

PS, vii, 15

August 14

Saint Maximilian Mary Kolbe, priest and martyr, Memorial

There is something so very dreadful, so satanic in tormenting those who never have harmed us, and who cannot defend themselves, who are utterly in our power, who have weapons neither of offence nor defence, that none but very hardened persons can endure the thought of it. Now this was just our Saviour's case: He had laid aside His glory, He had (as it were) disbanded His legions of Angels, He came on earth without arms, except the arms of truth, meekness, and righteousness, and committed Himself to the world in perfect innocence and sinlessness, and in utter helplessness, as the Lamb of God. In the words of St. Peter, "Who did no sin, neither was guile found in His mouth; who, when He was reviled, reviled not again; when He suffered, He threatened not; but committed Himself to Him that judgeth righteously." (1 Pet. Ii. 22, 23.)

PS, vii, 10

August 15

Assumption of the Blessed Virgin Mary, Solemnity

No limits but those proper to a creature can be assigned to the sanctity of Mary ... It was surely fitting then, it was becoming, that she should be taken up into heaven and not lie in the grave till Christ's second coming, who had passed a life of sanctity and of miracle such as hers. All the works of God are in a beautiful harmony; they are carried on to the end as they begin ... When one miracle is wrought, it may be expected to draw others after it for the completion of what is begun ... It would be a greater miracle if, her life being what it was, her death was like that of other men, than if it were such as to correspond to her life.

Mix., 18

August 16

Saint Stephen of Hungary, Optional Memorial

We are *ever* but beginning; the most perfect Christian is to himself but a beginner, a penitent prodigal, who has squandered God's gifts, and comes to Him to be tried over again, not as a son, but as a hired servant.

PS, iii, 7

August 17

How different is our state from that for which God made us. He meant us to be simple, and we are unreal ... And hence it is that the whole structure of society is so artificial; no one trusts another, if he can help it; safeguards, checks, and securities are ever sought after. No one means exactly what he says ... What, indeed, is the very function of society, as it is at present, but a rude attempt to cover the degradation of the fall, and to make men feel respect for themselves, and enjoy it in the eyes of others, without returning to God ... Men give good names to what is evil, they sanctify bad principles and feelings; and, knowing that there is vice and error, selfishness, pride, and ambition, in the world, they attempt, not to root out these evils, not to withstand these errors; – that they think a dream, the dream of theorists who do not know the world; – but to cherish and form alliance with them, to use them, to make a science of selfishness, to flatter and indulge error, and to bribe vice with the promise of bearing with it, so that it does but keep in the shade.

PS, viii, 18

August 18

The world is content with setting right the surface of things; the Church aims at regenerating the very depths of the heart. She ever begins with the beginning; and, as regards the multitude of her children, is never able to get beyond the beginning, but is continually employed in laying the foundation. She is engaged with what is essential, as previous and as introductory to the ornamental and the attractive. She is curing men and keeping them clear of mortal sin; she is "treating of justice and chastity, and the judgment to come:" she is insisting on faith and hope, and devotion, and honesty, and the elements of charity; and has so much to do with precept, that she almost leaves it to inspirations from Heaven to suggest what is of counsel and perfection. She aims at what is necessary rather than at what is desirable. She is for the many as well as for the few. She is putting souls in the way of salvation, that they may then be in a condition, if they shall be called upon, to aspire to the heroic, and to attain the full proportions, as well as the rudiments, of the beautiful.

Idea, 8

August 19

Saint John Eudes, priest, Optional Memorial

The firmest hold of theological truths is gained by habits of personal religion. When men begin all their works with the thought of God, acting for His sake, and to fulfil His will, when they ask His blessing on themselves and their life, pray to Him for the objects they desire, and see Him in the event, whether it be according to their prayers or not, they will find everything that happens tend to confirm them in the truths about Him which live in their imagination, varied and unearthly as those truths may be.

GA, 5.1

August 20

Saint Bernard of Clairvaux, abbot and doctor of the Church, Memorial

Religion has a store of wonderful secrets which no one can communicate to another ... Strange truths about ourselves, about God, about our duty, about the world, about heaven and hell, new modes of viewing things, discoveries which cannot be put into words, marvellous prospects and thoughts half understood, deep convictions inspiring joy and peace, these are a part of the revelation which Christ, the Son of God, brings to those who obey Him.

PS, vii, 9

August 21

Saint Pius X, pope, Memorial

We must transmit as we have received. We did not make the Church, we may not unmake it.

PS, iii, 14

August 22

Queenship of the Blessed Virgin Mary, Memorial

Mary ... as the Mother of our Lord, comes nearer to Him than any angel; nearer even than the Seraphim who surround Him, and cry continually, "Holy, Holy, Holy" ... The Blessed Mother of God has hosts of angels who do her service; and she is their Queen.

MD, 1.2.1

August 23

Saint Rose of Lima, virgin, Optional Memorial

Each good man has his own distinguishing grace, apart from the rest, his own particular hue and fragrance and fashion, as a flower may have. As, then, there are numberless flowers on the earth, all of them flowers, and so far like each other; and all springing from the same earth, and nourished by the same air and dew, and none without beauty; and yet some are more beautiful than others; and of those which are beautiful, some excel in colour and others in sweetness, and others in form; and then, again, those which are sweet have such perfect sweetness, yet so distinct, that we do not know how to compare them together, or to say which is the sweeter: so is it with souls filled and nurtured by God's secret grace.

PS, v, 6

August 24

Saint Bartholemew the Apostle, Feast

We need not give up our usual manner of life, in order to serve God; that the most humble and quietest station is acceptable to Him, if improved duly, – nay, affords means for maturing the highest Christian character, even that of an Apostle. Bartholomew read the Scriptures and prayed to God; and thus was trained at length to give up his life for Christ, when He demanded it.

PS, ii, 27

August 25

Saint Louis or Saint Joseph of Calasanz, priest, Optional Memorial

There is a physical beauty and a moral: there is a beauty of person, there is a beauty of our moral being, which is natural virtue; and in like manner there is a beauty, there is a perfection, of the intellect.

Idea, 1.5

August 26

[The] perfection of the Intellect ... is the clear, calm, accurate vision and comprehension of all things, as far as the finite mind can embrace them, each in its place, and with its own character-istics upon it. It is almost prophetic from its knowledge of history; it is almost heart-searching from its knowledge of human nature; it has almost supernatural charity from its freedom from littleness and prejudice; it has almost the repose of faith, because nothing can startle it; it has almost the beauty and harmony of heavenly contemplation, so intimate is it with the eternal order of things and the music of the spheres.

Idea, 1.6

August 27

Saint Monica, Memorial

Many a mother who is anxious for her son's bodily welfare, neglects his soul. So did not the Saint of today; her son might be accomplished, eloquent, able, and distinguished; all this was nothing to her while he was dead in God's sight, while he was the slave of sin, while he was the prey of heresy. She desired his true life. She wearied heaven with prayer, and wore out herself with praying; she did not at once prevail. He left his home; he was carried forward by his four bearers, ignorance, pride, appetite, and ambition; he was carried out into a foreign land, he crossed over from Africa to Italy. She followed him, she followed the corpse, the chief, the only mourner; she went where he went, from city to city. It was nothing to her to leave her dear home and her native soil; she had no country below; her sole rest, her sole repose, her *Nunc dimittis*, was his new birth. So while she still walked forth in her deep anguish and isolation, and her silent prayer, she was at length rewarded by the long-coveted miracle. Grace melted the proud heart, and purified the corrupt breast of Augustine, and restored and comforted his mother.

OS, 1

August 28

Saint Augustine, bishop and doctor, Memorial

St. Augustine ... has formed the intellect of Christian Europe.

Apo., 5

August 29

The Beheading of Saint John the Baptist, martyr, Memorial

The foundations of the ocean, the vast realms of water which girdle the earth, are as tranquil and as silent in the storm as in a calm. So is it with the souls of holy men. They have a well of peace springing up within them unfathomable.

PS, v, 5

August 30

Our duty lies in acts – acts of course of every kind, acts of the mind, as well as of the tongue, or of the hand; but anyhow, it lies mainly in acts; it does not directly lie in moods or feelings. He who aims at praying well, loving sincerely, disputing meekly, as the respective duties occur, is wise and religious; but he who aims vaguely and generally at being in a spiritual frame of mind, is entangled in a deceit of words ... Let us do our duty as it presents itself; this is the secret of true faith and peace.

PS, ii, 14

August 31

In this ... consists our whole duty, first in contemplating Almighty God, as in Heaven, so in our hearts and souls; and next, while we contemplate Him, in acting towards and for Him in the works of every day; in viewing by faith His glory without and within us, and in acknowledging it by our obedience. Thus we shall unite conceptions the most lofty concerning His majesty and bounty towards us, with the most lowly, minute, and unostentatious service to Him.

PS, iii, 18

September

September 1

The more we are forbidden violence, the more we are exhorted to prudence ... "Be ye wise as serpents," He said; then, knowing how dangerous such wisdom is, especially in times of temptation, if a severe conscientiousness is not awake, He added, "and harmless as doves" ... Not only is harmlessness the corrective of wisdom, securing it against the corruption of craft and deceit, as stated in the text; but innocence, simplicity, implicit obedience to God, tranquillity of mind, contentment, these and the like virtues are themselves a sort of wisdom; – I mean, they produce the same results as wisdom, because God works for those who do not work for themselves; and thus Christians especially incur the charge of craft at the hands of the world, because they pretend to so little, yet effect so much.

SD, 20

September 2

St. Peter ... is no recluse, no solitary student, no dreamer about the past, no doter upon the dead and gone, no projector of the visionary. He for eighteen hundred years has lived in the world; he has seen all fortunes, he has encountered all adversaries, he has shaped himself for all emergencies ... He came first upon an age of refinement and luxury like our own, and, in spite of the persecutor, fertile in the resources of his cruelty, he soon gathered, out of all classes of society, the slave, the soldier, the high-born lady, and the sophist, materials enough to form a people to his Master's honour. The savage hordes came down in torrents from the north, and Peter went out to meet them, and by his very eye he sobered them, and backed them in their full career. They turned aside and flooded the whole earth, but only to be more surely civilized by him, and to be made ten times more his children even than the older populations which they had overwhelmed. Lawless kings arose, sagacious as the Roman, passionate as the Hun, yet in him they found their match, and were shattered, and he lived on. The gates of the earth were opened to the east and west, and men poured out to take possession; but he went with them by his missionaries, to China, to Mexico, carried along by zeal and charity, as far as those children of men were led by enterprise, covetousness, or ambition. Has he failed in his successes up to this hour? Did he, in our fathers' day, fail in his struggle with Joseph of Germany and his confederates, with Napoleon, a greater name, and his dependent kings, that, though in another kind of fight, he should fail in ours? What grey hairs are on the head of Judah, whose youth is renewed like the eagle's, whose feet are like the feet of harts, and underneath the Everlasting arms?

Idea, 1.1

September 3

Saint Gregory the Great, pope and doctor, Memorial

A great Pontiff must be detached from everything save the deposit of faith, the tradition of the Apostles, and the vital principles of the divine polity ... The Popes have never found any difficulty, when the proper moment came, of following out a new and daring line of policy ... of leaving the old world to shift for itself and to disappear from the scene in its due season, and of fastening on and establishing themselves in the new ... [Consider] St Gregory's behaviour to the Anglo-Saxon race, on the break-up of the old civilization ... With what pertinacity of zeal does Gregory send his missionaries to England! with what an appetite he waits for the tidings of their progress! with what a relish he dwells over the good news, when they are able to send it! ... What were these outer barbarians to Gregory? how could they relieve him or profit him? What compensation could they make for what the Church was then losing, or might lose in future?

HS, iii, 1.11

September 4

The theologian, speaking of Divine Omnipotence, for the time simply ignores the laws of nature as existing restraints upon its exercise; and the physical philosopher, on the other hand, in his experiments upon natural phenomena, is simply ascertaining those laws, putting aside the question of that Omnipotence. If the theologian, in tracing the ways of Providence, were stopped with objections grounded on the impossibility of physical miracles, he would justly protest against the interruption; and were the philosopher, who was determining the motion of the heavenly bodies, to be questioned about their Final or their First Cause, he too would suffer an illogical interruption. The latter asks the cause of volcanoes, and is impatient at being told it is "the divine vengeance;" the former asks the cause of the overthrow of the guilty cities, and is preposterously referred to the volcanic action still visible in their neighbourhood. The inquiry into final causes for the moment passes over the existence of established laws; the inquiry into physical, passes over for the moment the existence of God. In other words, physical science is in a certain sense atheistic, for the very reason it is not theology.

Idea, 1.9

September 5

The system of Nature is just as much connected with Religion, where minds are not religious, as a watch or a steam-carriage. The material world, indeed, is infinitely more wonderful than any human contrivance; but wonder is not religion, or we should be worshipping our railroads. What the physical creation presents to us in itself is a piece of machinery, and when men speak of a Divine Intelligence as its Author, this god of theirs is not the Living and True, unless the spring is the god of a watch, or steam the creator of the engine. Their idol, taken at advantage (though it is *not* an idol, for they do not worship it), is the animating principle of a vast and complicated system; it is subjected to laws, and it is connatural and co-extensive with matter ... It is an instinct, or a soul of the world, or a vital power; it is not the Almighty God.

DA, 4.7

September 6

The philosopher aspires towards a divine *principle*; the Christian, towards a Divine *Agent*. Now, dedication of our energies to the service of a person is the occasion of the highest and most noble virtues, disinterested attachment, self-devotion, loyalty; habitual humility, moreover, from the knowledge that there must ever be one that is above us. On the other hand, in whatever degree we approximate towards a mere standard of excellence, we do not really advance towards it, but bring it to us; the excellence we venerate becomes part of ourselves – we become a god to ourselves.

US, 2

September 7

Science gives us the grounds or premises from which religious truths are to be inferred; but it does not set about inferring them, much less does it reach the inference; – that is not its province. It brings before us phenomena, and it leaves us, if we will, to call them works of design, wisdom, or benevolence; and further still, if we will, to proceed to confess an Intelligent Creator. We have to take its facts, and to give them a meaning, and to draw our own conclusions from them. First comes Knowledge, then a view, then reasoning, and then belief. This is why Science has so little of a religious tendency; deductions have no power of persuasion. The heart is commonly reached, not through the reason, but through the imagination, by means of direct impressions, by the testimony of facts and events, by history, by description. Persons influence us, voices melt us, looks subdue us, deeds inflame us. Many a man will live and die upon a dogma: no man will be a martyr for a conclusion ... No one, I say, will die for his own calculations; he dies for realities. This is why a literary religion is so little to be depended upon; it looks well in fair weather, but its doctrines are opinions, and, when called to suffer for them, it slips them between its folios, or burns them at its hearth ... After all, man is *not* a reasoning animal; he is a seeing, feeling, contemplating, acting animal. He is influenced by what is direct and precise. It is very well to freshen our impressions and convictions from physics, but to create them we must go elsewhere.

DA, 4.6

September 8

Birth of the Blessed Virgin Mary, Feast

How did Mary become the *Rosa Mystica*, the choice, delicate, perfect flower of God's spiritual creation? It was by being born, nurtured and sheltered in the mystical garden or Paradise of God. Scripture makes use of the figure of a garden, when it would speak of heaven and its blessed inhabitants ... Such was the garden in which the Mystical Rose, the Immaculate Mary, was sheltered and nursed to be the Mother of the All Holy God, from her birth to her espousals to St. Joseph, a term of thirteen years. For three years of it she was in the arms of her holy mother, St. Anne, and then for ten years she lived in the temple of God. In those blessed gardens, as they may be called, she lived by herself, continually visited by the dew of God's grace, and growing up a more and more heavenly flower, till at the end of that period she was meet for the inhabitation in her of the Most Holy ... When the angel Gabriel had to come to her, he found her "full of grace," which had, from her good use of it, accumulated in her from the first moment of her being.

MD, 1.1.5.2

September 9

Saint Peter Claver, priest, Optional Memorial

We were made for action, and for right action, – for thought, and for true thought. Let us live while we live; let us be alive and doing; let us act on what we have, since we have not what we wish. Let us believe what we do not see and know. Let us forestall knowledge by faith. Let us maintain before we have demonstrated. This seeming paradox is the secret of happiness.

DA, 3.6

September 10

Many ... of those unhappy men who have denied the Christian faith, treat the religious principle altogether as a mere unnatural, eccentric state of mind, a peculiar untoward condition of the affections to which weakness will reduce a man, whether it has been brought on by anxiety, oppressive sorrow, bodily disease, excess of imagination or the like, and temporary or permanent according to the circumstances of the disposing cause; a state to which we all are liable, as we are liable to any other mental injury, but unmanly and unworthy of our dignity as rational beings.

PS, vii, 2

September 11

I wish the intellect to range with the utmost freedom, and religion to enjoy an equal freedom; but ... it will not satisfy me ... to have two independent systems, intellectual and religious, going at once side by side, by a sort of division of labour, and only accidentally brought together.

OS, 1

September 12

Holy Name of the Blessed Virgin Mary, Optional Memorial

O Almighty God, who seest how earnestly we desire to place ourselves under the shadow of the name of Mary, vouchsafe, we beseech Thee, that as often as we invoke her in our need, we may receive grace and pardon from Thy holy heaven, through Christ our Lord.

MD, 2 'Litany of Holy Name of Mary'

September 13

Saint John Chrysostom, bishop and doctor, Memorial

I consider St. Chrysostom's charm to lie in his intimate sympathy and compassionateness for the whole world, not only in its strength, but in its weakness; in the lively regard with which he views every thing that comes before him, taken in the concrete ... the interest which he takes in all things, not so far as God has made them alike, but as He has made them different from each other ... the discriminating affectionateness with which he accepts every one for what is personal in him and unlike others ... Possessed though he be by the fire of divine charity, he has not lost one fibre, he does not miss one vibration, of the complicated whole of human sentiment and affection; like the miraculous bush in the desert, which, for all the flame that wrapt it round, was not thereby consumed.

HS, ii, 2.5

September 14

Triumph of the Holy Cross, Feast

Those who in the Cross of Christ see the Atonement for sin, cannot choose but glory in it; and its mysteriousness does but make them glory in it the more.

PS, iii, 12

September 15

Our Lady of Sorrows, Memorial

What an overwhelming horror it must have been for the Blessed Mary to witness the Passion and the Crucifixion of her Son! Her anguish was, as Holy Simeon had announced to her, at the time of that Son's Presentation in the Temple, a sword piercing her soul ... She [is] most truly the Queen of *Martyrs*.

MD, 1.3.1

September 16

Saints Cornelius, pope, and Cyprian, bishop, martyrs, Memorial

St. Cyprian ... loved Christianity well enough to give up for it at a mature age secular engagements, settled habits and opinions, property, quiet, and at length life itself.

Preface to the *Treatises of S. Cæcilius Cyprian*

September 17

Saint Robert Bellarmine, bishop and doctor, Optional Memorial

Sentiment, whether imaginative or emotional, falls back upon the intellect for its stay, when sense cannot be called into exercise; and it is in this way that devotion falls back upon dogma.

GA, 5.1

September 18

Religion, as a mere sentiment, is to me a dream and a mockery. As well can there be filial love without the fact of a father, as devotion without the fact of a Supreme Being.

Apo., 2

September 19

Saint Januarius, bishop and martyr, Optional Memorial

[Catholics] affirm that the Supreme Being has wrought miracles on earth ever since the time of the Apostles: Protestants deny it ...

Both they and we start with the miracles of the Apostles; and then their First Principle or presumption, against our miracles, is this, "What God did once, He is *not* likely to do again;" while our First Principle or presumption, for our miracles, is this, "What God did once, He *is* likely to do again" ... Bring before the Protestant the largest mass of evidence and testimony in proof of the miraculous liquefaction of St. Januarius's blood at Naples, let him be urged by witnesses of the highest character, chemists of the first fame, circumstances the most favourable for the detection of imposture, coincidences, and confirmations the most close and minute and indirect, he will not believe it; his First Principle *blocks* belief ...

Catholics ... hold the mystery of the Incarnation; and the Incarnation is the most stupendous event which ever can take place on earth; and after it and henceforth, I do not see how we can scruple at any miracle on the mere ground of its being unlikely to happen. No miracle can be so great as that which took place in the Holy House of Nazareth ... More is plain too. Miracles are not only not unlikely, they are positively likely; and for this simple reason, because, for the most part, when God begins He goes on. We conceive that when He first did a miracle, He began a series; what He commenced, He continued: what has been, will be ... This beautiful world of nature, His own work, He broke its harmony; He broke through His own laws which He had imposed on it; He worked out His purposes, not simply through it, but in violation of it ... If Divine Wisdom would not leave an infringement, an anomaly, a solecism on His work, He might be expected to introduce a series of miracles, and turn the apparent exception into an additional law of His providence. If the Divine Being does a thing once, He is, judging by human reason, likely to do it again.

Prepos., 7

September 20

Saint Andrew Kim Taegon, priest, and Paul Chong Hasang and companions, martyrs, Memorial

Error may flourish for a time, but Truth will prevail in the end. The only effect of error ultimately is to promote Truth.

Idea, 2.8

September 21

Saint Matthew the Evangelist, Feast

All men may read or hear the Gospels, and in knowing them, they will know all that is necessary to be known in order to feel aright; they will know all that any one knows, all that has been told us, all that the greatest saints have ever had to make them full of love and sacred fear.

PS, vii, 10

September 22

It should not surprise us when men of acute and powerful understandings more or less reject the Gospel, for this reason, that the Christian revelation addresses itself to our hearts, to our love of truth and goodness, our fear of sinning, and our desire to gain God's favour; and quickness, sagacity, depth of thought, strength of mind, power of comprehension, perception of the beautiful, power of language, and the like, though they are excellent gifts, are clearly quite of a different kind from these spiritual excellences – a man may have the one without having the other.

PS, viii, 13

September 23

Saint Pio of Pietrelcina, priest, Memorial

One living Saint, though there be but one, is a pledge of the whole Church Invisible.

PS, iii, 17

September 24

"*Securus judicat orbis terrarum.*" ... These words again and again ... kept ringing in my ears. "*Securus judicat orbis terrarum*" ... What a light was hereby thrown upon every controversy in the Church! ... The deliberate judgment, in which the whole Church at length rests and acquiesces, is an infallible prescription and a final sentence against such portions of it as protest and secede. Who can account for the impressions which are made on him? For a mere sentence, the words of St. Augustine, struck me with a power which I never had felt from any words before. To take a familiar instance, they were like the "Turn again Whittington" of the chime; or, to take a more serious one, they were like the "*Tolle, lege, – Tolle, lege,*" of the child, which converted St. Augustine himself. "*Securus judicat orbis terrarum*!" ... I had seen the shadow of a hand upon the wall. It was clear that I had a good deal to learn on the question of the Churches, and that perhaps some new light was coming upon me. He who has seen a ghost, cannot be as if he had never seen it. The heavens had opened and closed again. The thought for the moment had been, "The Church of Rome will be found right after all;" and then it had vanished.

Apo., 3

September 25

Newman's last sermon as an Anglican, 'The Parting of Friends', 1843

O loving friends, should you know any one whose lot it has been, by writing or by word of mouth, in some degree to help you ... if he has ever told you what you knew about yourselves, or what you did not know; has read to you your wants or feelings, and comforted you by the very reading; has made you feel that there was a higher life than this daily one, and a brighter world than that you see; or encouraged you, or sobered you, or opened a way to the inquiring, or soothed the perplexed; if what he has said or done has ever made you take interest in him, and feel well inclined towards him; remember such a one in time to come, though you hear him not, and pray for him, that in all things he may know God's will, and at all times he may be ready to fulfil it.

SD, 26

September 26

Saints Cosmas and Damian, martyrs, Optional Memorial

What ... is it that we who profess religion lack? ... This: a willingness to be changed, a willingness to suffer (if I may use such a word), to suffer Almighty God to change us. We do not like to let go our old selves ... We feel as if we should not *be* ourselves any longer.

PS, v, 17

September 27

Saint Vincent de Paul, priest, Memorial

How many are the souls, in distress, anxiety or loneliness, whose one need is to find a being to whom they can pour out their feelings unheard by the world? Tell them out they must; they cannot tell them out to those whom they see every hour. They want to tell them and not to tell them; and they want to tell them out, yet be as if they be not told; they wish to tell them to one who is strong enough to bear them, yet not too strong to despise them; they wish to tell them to one who can at once advise and can sympathize with them; they wish to relieve themselves of a load, to gain a solace, to receive the assurance that there is one who thinks of them, and one to whom in thought they can recur, to whom they can betake themselves, if necessary, from time to time, while they are in the world ... If there is a heavenly idea in the Catholic Church, looking at it simply as an idea, surely, next after the Blessed Sacrament, Confession is such.

Prepos., 8

September 28

Saints Lorenzo Ruiz and companions, martyrs, Memorial

If we follow the voice of God, shall be brought on step by step into a new world, of which before we had no idea.

PS, viii, 13

September 29

Saints Michael, Gabriel, and Raphael, Archangels, Feast

As our souls move our bodies ... so there are Spiritual Intelligences which move those wonderful and vast portions of the natural world which seem to be inanimate; and as the gestures, speech, and expressive countenances of our friends around us enable us to hold intercourse with them, so in the motions of universal Nature, in the interchange of day and night, summer and winter, wind and storm, fulfilling His word, we are reminded of the blessed and dutiful Angels ... Every breath of air and ray of light and heat, every beautiful prospect, is, as it were, the skirts of their garments, the waving of the robes of those whose faces see God in heaven.

PS, ii, 29

September 30

Saint Jerome, priest and doctor, Memorial

There are two attributes of the Bible throughout ... attributes which, while at first sight in contrast, have a sort of necessary connexion, and set off each other – simplicity and depth. Simplicity leads a writer to say things without display; and depth obliges him to use inadequate words. Scripture then, treating of invisible things, at best must use words less than those things; and, as if from a feeling that no words can be worthy of them, it does not condescend to use even the strongest that exist, but often take the plainest. The deeper the thought, the plainer the word; the word and thought diverge from each other. Again, it is a property of depth to lead a writer into verbal contradictions; and it is a property of simplicity not to care to avoid them. Again, when a writer is deep, his half sentences, parentheses, clauses, nay his words, have a meaning in them independent of the context, and admit of exposition. There is nothing put in for ornament's sake, or for rhetoric; nothing put in for the mere sake of anything else, but all for its own sake; all as the expressions and shadows of great things, as seeds of thought, and with corresponding realities.

DA, 3.5

October

October 1

Saint Therese of the Child Jesus, virgin and doctor, Memorial

Eternal God ... *because* He is eternal, is ever *young*.

MD, 1.1.6

October 2

Guardian Angels, Memorial

> *My oldest friend, mine from the hour*
> *   When first I drew my breath;*
> *My faithful friend, that shall be mine,*
> *   Unfailing, till my death ...*
>
> *Mine, when I stand before the Judge;*
> *   And mine, if spared to stay*
> *Within the golden furnace, till*
> *   My sin is burn'd away.*
>
> *And mine, O Brother of my soul,*
> *   When my release shall come;*
> *Thy gentle arms shall lift me then,*
> *   Thy wings shall waft me home.*

VV, 'Guardian Angel'

October 3

A thick black veil is spread between this world and the next. We mortal men range up and down it, to and fro, and see nothing. There is no access through it into the next world. In the Gospel this veil is not removed; it remains, but every now and then marvellous disclosures are made to us of what is behind it. At times we seem to catch a glimpse of a Form which we shall hereafter see face to face. We approach, and in spite of the darkness, our hands, or our head, or our brow, or our lips become, as it were, sensible of the contact of something more than earthly. We know not where we are, but we have been bathing in water, and a voice tells us that it is blood. Or we have a mark signed upon our foreheads, and it spake of Calvary. Or we recollect a hand laid upon our heads, and surely it had the print of nails in it, and resembled His who with a touch gave sight to the blind and raised the dead. Or we have been eating and drinking; and it was not a dream surely, that One fed us from His wounded side, and renewed our nature by the heavenly meat He gave. Thus in many ways He, who is Judge to us, prepares us to be judged, – He, who is to glorify us, prepares us to be glorified, that He may not take us unawares; but that when the voice of the Archangel sounds, and we are called to meet the Bridegroom, we may be ready.

PS, v, 1

October 4

Saint Francis of Assisi

[Angel to Gerontius]
There was a mortal, who is now above
In the mid glory: he, when near to die,
Was given communion with the Crucified, –
Such, that the Master's very wounds were stamp'd
Upon his flesh; and, from the agony
Which thrill'd through body and soul in that embrace
Learn that the flame of the Everlasting Love
Doth burn ere it transform ...

VV, 'Dream of Gerontius'

October 5

When we contemplate Christ as manifested in the Gospels, the Christ who exists therein, external to our own imaginings, and who is as really a living being, and sojourned on earth as truly as any of us, then we shall at length believe in Him with a conviction, a confidence, and an entireness, which can no more be annihilated than the belief in our senses. It is impossible for a Christian mind to meditate on the Gospels, without feeling, beyond all manner of doubt, that He who is the subject of them is God.

PS, iii, 10

October 6

Saint Bruno, priest, Optional Memorial

The existence of fear in religion does not depend on the circumstance of our being sinners; it is short of that. Were we pure as the Angels, yet in His sight, one should think, we could not but fear, before whom the heavens are not clean, nor the Angels free from folly. The Seraphim themselves veiled their faces while they cried, Glory! Even then were it true that sin was not a great evil, or was no great evil in us, nevertheless the mere circumstance that God is infinite and all-perfect is an overwhelming thought to creatures and mortal men, and ought to lead all persons who profess religion to profess also religious fear.

PS, v, 2

October 7

Our Lady of the Rosary, Memorial

The glories of Mary are for the sake of Jesus ... We praise and bless her as the first of creatures, that we may confess Him as our sole Creator.

Mix., 17

October 8

Lead, Kindly Light, amid the encircling gloom
      Lead Thou me on!
The night is dark, and I am far from home –
      Lead Thou me on!
Keep Thou my feet; I do not ask to see
The distant scene – one step enough for me.

I was not ever thus, nor pray'd that Thou
      Shouldst lead me on.
I loved to choose and see my path, but now
      Lead Thou me on!
I loved the garish day, and, spite of fears,
Pride ruled my will: remember not past years.

So long Thy power hath blest me, sure it still
      Will lead me on,
O'er moor and fen, o'er crag and torrent, till
      The night is gone;
And with the morn those angel faces smile
Which I have loved long since, and lost awhile.

VV, 'The Pillar of the Cloud'

October 9

Blessed John Henry Newman, Optional Memorial

Newman received into the Catholic Church, 1845

> *Praise to the Holiest in the height*
> *And in the depth be praise:*
> *In all His words most wonderful;*
> *Most sure in all His ways!*

VV, 'Dream of Gerontius'

October 10

True religion is the summit and perfection of false religions: it combines in one whatever there is of good and true, severally remaining in each. And in like manner the Catholic Creed is for the most part the combination of separate truths which heretics have divided among themselves, and err in dividing. So that, in matter of fact, if a religious mind were educated in and sincerely attached to some form of heathenism or heresy, and then were brought under the light of truth, it would be drawn off from error into the truth, not by losing what it had, but by gaining what it had not, – not by being unclothed, but by being "clothed upon," "that mortality may be swallowed up of life." That same principle of faith which attaches it to its original human teaching, would attach it to the truth; and that portion of its original teaching which was to be cast off as absolutely false, would not be directly rejected, but indirectly rejected *in* the reception of the truth which is its opposite. True conversion is of a positive, not a negative character.

DA, 3.6

October 11

You must come ... to the Church to learn; you must come, not to bring your own notions to her, but with the intention of ever being a learner; you must come with the intention of taking her for your portion, and of never leaving her.

Mix., 11

October 12

When men change their religious opinions really and truly, it is not merely their opinions that they change, but their hearts; and this evidently is not done in a moment.

PS, viii, 15

October 13

Real assents ... are of a personal character, each individual having his own, and being known by them.

GA, 4.2

October 14

Saint Callistus I, pope and martyr, Optional Memorial

It is the concrete being that reasons; pass a number of years, and I find my mind in a new place; how? the whole man moves; paper logic is but the record of it.

Apo., 4

October 15

Saint Teresa of Jesus, virgin and doctor, Memorial

There is an inward world, which none see but those who belong to it ... an inward world into which they enter who come near to Christ.

PS, v, 20

October 16

Saint Hedwig, religious, or Saint Margaret Mary Alcoque, virgin, Optional Memorial

O my God, I do not know what infinity means – but one thing I see, that Thou art loving to a depth and height far beyond any measurement of mine.

MD, 3.10

October 17

Saint Ignatius of Antioch, bishop and martyr, Optional Memorial

Ignatius considers our life and salvation to lie, not in the Atonement by itself, but in the Incarnation; but neither in the Incarnation nor Atonement as past events, but, as present facts, in an existing mode, in which our Saviour comes to us; or, to speak more plainly, in our Saviour Himself who is God in our flesh, and not only so, but in flesh which has been offered up on the Cross in sacrifice, which has died and has risen.

Ess., i, 6

October 18

Saint Luke the Evangelist, Feast

St. Luke differed from his fellow-evangelists and fellow-disciples in having received the advantages of (what is called) a liberal education ... The *danger* of an elegant and polite education is, that it separates feeling and acting; it teaches us to think, speak, and be affected aright, without forcing us to practise what is right ... But St. Luke and St. Paul show us, that we may be sturdy workers in the Lord's service, and bear our cross manfully, though we be adorned with all the learning of the Egyptians; or rather, that the resources of literature, and the graces of a cultivated mind, may be made both a lawful source of enjoyment to the possessor, and a means of introducing and recommending the Truth to others.

PS, ii, 30

October 19

Saints Jean de Brébeuf, Isaac Jogues, priest and companions, martyrs, or Saint Paul of the Cross, priest, Optional Memorial

The mere fact of our saying more than we feel is not necessarily sinful. St. Peter did not rise up to the full meaning of his confession, "Thou art the Christ," yet he was pronounced blessed. St. James and St. John said, "We are able," without clear apprehension, yet without offence. We ever promise things greater than we master, and we wait on God to enable us to perform them. Our promising involves a prayer for light and strength. And so again we all say the

Creed, but who comprehends it fully? All we can hope is, that we are in the way to understand it; that we partly understand it; that we desire, pray, and strive to understand it more and more. Our Creed becomes a sort of prayer.

PS, v, 3

October 20

The body of the faithful is one of the witnesses to the fact of the tradition of revealed doctrine, and ... their *consensus* through Christendom is the voice of the Infallible Church ... The tradition of the Apostles, committed to the whole Church in its various constituents and functions *per modum unius*, manifests itself variously at various times: sometimes by the mouth of the episcopacy, sometimes by the doctors, sometimes by the people, sometimes by liturgies, rites, ceremonies, and customs, by events, disputes, movements, and all those other phenomena which are comprised under the name of history. It follows that none of these channels of tradition may be treated with disrespect; granting at the same time fully, that the gift of discerning, discriminating, defining, promulgating, and enforcing any portion of that tradition resides solely in the *Ecclesia docens* ...

The *Ecclesia docens* is more happy when she has ... enthusiastic partisans about her ... than when she cuts off the faithful from the study of her divine doctrines and the sympathy of her divine contemplations, and requires from them *fides implicita* in her word, which in the educated classes will terminate in indifference, and in the poorer in superstition.

'On Consulting the Faithful in Matters of Doctrine'

October 21

Our Lord ... is Prophet, Priest, and King; and after His pattern, and in human measure, Holy Church has a triple office too ... three offices, which are indivisible, though diverse, viz. teaching, rule, and sacred ministry ... Christianity, then, is at once a philosophy, a political power, and a religious rite: as a religion, it is Holy; as a philosophy, it is Apostolic; as a political power, it is imperial, that is, One and Catholic. As a religion, its special centre of action is pastor and flock; as a philosophy, the Schools; as a rule, the Papacy and its Curia ... Arduous as are the duties involved in these three offices, to discharge one by one, much more arduous are they to administer, when taken in combination. Each of the three has its separate scope and direction; each has its own interests to promote and further; each has to find room for the claims of the other two; and each will find its own line of action influenced and modified by the others, nay, sometimes in a particular case the necessity of the others converted into a rule of duty for itself ...

Theology is the fundamental and regulating principle of the whole Church system. It is commensurate with Revelation, and Revelation is the initial and essential idea of Christianity ... Yet theology cannot always have its own way; it is too hard, too intellectual, too exact, to be always equitable, or to be always compassionate; and it sometimes has a conflict or overthrow, or has to consent to a truce or a compromise, in consequence of the rival force of religious sentiment or ecclesiastical interests.

VM, i, 'Preface to the Third Edition'

October 22

When we consider the succession of ages during which the Catholic system has endured, the severity of the trials it has undergone, the sudden and wonderful changes without and within which have befallen it, the incessant mental activity and the intellectual gifts of its maintainers, the enthusiasm which it has kindled, the fury of the controversies which have been carried on among its professors, the impetuosity of the assaults made upon it, the ever-increasing responsibilities to which it has been committed by the continuous development of its dogmas, it is quite inconceivable that it should not have been broken up and lost, were it a corruption of Christianity. Yet it is still living, if there be a living religion or philosophy in the world; vigorous, energetic, persuasive, progressive; *vires acquirit eundo*; it grows and is not overgrown; it spreads out, yet is not enfeebled; it is ever germinating, yet ever consistent with itself.

Dev., 12

October 23

Saint John of Capistrano, priest, Optional Memorial

Our Lord ... founded not merely a religion, but (what was then quite a new idea in the world) a system of religious warfare, an aggressive and militant body, a dominant Catholic Church, which aimed at the benefit of all nations by the spiritual conquest of all; and ... this warfare, then begun by it, has gone on without cessation down to this day, and now is as living and real as ever it was.

GA, 10.2

October 24

Saint Anthony Mary Claret, bishop, Optional Memorial

Christ's kingdom, though a visible temporal kingdom, is *in* this world, but not *of* this world, and is maintained by weapons, not carnal, but heavenly ... We conquer by turning the cheek to the smiter; by repaying good for evil; by praying for the persecutor; by giving to him that asks; by suffering for the feeble; by sheltering the widow and the fatherless; by being champions of the poor; by fortitude, firmness, constancy, disinterestedness, fairness, moderation, nobleness, bountifulness, self-sacrifice, and self-command; by patience in enduring ill, and perseverance in doing well.

SD, 17

October 25

It has often happened that, because the elect are few, serious men have considered that this took place in consequence of some fixed decree of God ... [but] if you say that God does absolutely choose the one and reject the other, then *that* becomes the mystery. You do but throw it back a step. It is as difficult to explain this absolute willing or not willing, on the part of Almighty God, as to account for the existence of free will in man. It is as inexplicable why God should act differently towards this man and that, as it is why this man or that should act differently towards God. On the other hand, we are solemnly assured in Scripture that God "hath no pleasure in the death of the wicked;" that He is "not willing that any should perish, but that all should come to repentance." (Ezek. xxxiii. 11. 2 Pet. iii. 9.)

PS, v, 18

October 26

We do not know the *standard* by which God will judge us. Nothing that we are can assure us that we shall answer to what He expects of us; for we do not know what that is; what we are can but cheer us and give us hopes and good spirits.

PS, v, 18

October 27

Our sins are more in number than the hairs of our head; yet even the hairs of our head are all numbered by Him. He counts our sins, and, as He counts, so can He forgive; for that reckoning, great though it be, comes to an end; but His mercies fail not, and His Son's merits are infinite.

PS, v, 19

October 28

Saint Simon and Saint Jude, apostles, Feast

To hope is, not only to believe in God, but to believe and be certain that He loves us and means well to us; and therefore it is a great Christian grace.

CS, 1

October 29

Eye of man hath not seen the face of God; and heart of man could never have conceived or invented so wonderful a manifestation, as the Gospel contains, of His ineffable, overwhelming Attributes. I believe the infinite condescension of the Highest to be true, because it has been imagined.

OS, 6

October 30

Rationalism is a certain abuse of Reason; that is, a use of it for purposes for which it never was intended, and is unfitted. To rationalize in matters of Revelation is to make our reason the standard and measure of the doctrines revealed; to stipulate that those doctrines should be such as to carry with them their own justification; to reject them, if they come in collision with our existing opinions or habits of thought, or are with difficulty harmonized with our existing stock of knowledge. And thus a rationalistic spirit is the antagonist of Faith; for Faith is, in its very nature, the acceptance of what our reason cannot reach, simply and absolutely upon testimony.

Ess., i, 2.1

October 31

Suppose that the three first Gospels are an accidental collection of traditions or legends, for which no one is responsible, and in which Christians had faith because there was nothing else to put faith in. This is the limit to which extreme scepticism can proceed, and we are willing to commence our argument by granting it. Still, starting at this disadvantage, we should be prepared to argue, that if, in spite of this, and after all, there be shadowed out in these anonymous and fortuitous documents a Teacher *sui generis*, distinct, consistent, and original, then does that picture, thus accidentally resulting, for the very reason of its accidental composition, only become more marvellous; then is He an historical fact, and again a supernatural or divine fact; – historical from the consistency of the representation, and because the time cannot be assigned when it was not received as a reality; and supernatural, in proportion as the qualities with which He is invested in those writings are incompatible with what it is reasonable or possible to ascribe to human nature viewed simply in itself.

DA, 6

November

November 1

All Saints

Very various are the Saints, their very variety is a token of God's workmanship; but however various, and whatever was their special line of duty, they have been heroes in it; they have attained such noble self-command, they have so crucified the flesh, they have so renounced the world; they are so meek, so gentle, so tender-hearted, so merciful, so sweet, so cheerful, so full of prayer, so diligent, so forgetful of injuries; they have sustained such great and continued pains, they have persevered in such vast labours, they have made such valiant confessions, they have wrought such abundant miracles, they have been blessed with such strange successes, that they have been the means of setting up a standard before us of truth, of magnanimity, of holiness, of love. They are not always our examples, we are not always bound to follow them; not more than we are bound to obey literally some of our Lord's precepts, such as turning the cheek or giving away the coat; not more than we can follow the course of the sun, moon, or stars in the heavens; but, though not always our examples, they are always our standard of right and good; they are raised up to be monuments and lessons, they remind us of God, they introduce us into the unseen world, they teach us what Christ loves, they track out for us the way which leads heavenward.

Mix., 5

November 2

All Souls

O God of the Spirits of all flesh, O Jesu, Lover of souls, we recommend unto Thee the souls of all those Thy servants, who have departed with the sign of faith and sleep the sleep of peace. We beseech Thee, O Lord and Saviour, that, as in Thy mercy to them Thou becamest man, so now Thou wouldest hasten the time, and admit them to Thy presence above ... May the heavens be opened to them, and the Angels rejoice with them ... May all the Saints and elect of God, who in this world suffered torments for Thy Name, befriend them; that, being freed from the prison beneath, they may be admitted into the glories of that kingdom, where with the Father and the Holy Ghost Thou livest and reignest one God, world without end ... Eternal rest give to them, O Lord. And may perpetual light shine on them.

MD, 2, 'Prayer for the Faithful Departed'

November 3

Saint Martin de Porres, religious, Optional Memorial

Nothing is so rare as honesty and singleness of mind; so much so, that a person who is really honest, is already perfect.

PS, v, 3

November 4

Saint Charles Borromeo, bishop, Memorial

The Catholic Church allows no image of any sort, material or immaterial, no dogmatic symbol, no rite, no sacrament, no Saint, not even the Blessed Virgin herself, to come between the soul and its Creator. It is face to face, '*solus cum solo*', in all matters between man and his God.

Apo., 4

November 5

Do you know what it is to be in anxiety lest something should happen which may happen or may not, or to be in suspense about some important event, which makes your heart beat when you are reminded of it, and of which you think the first thing in the morning? Do you know what it is to have a friend in a distant country, to expect news of him, and to wonder from day to day what he is now doing, and whether he is well? Do you know what it is so to live upon a person who is present with you, that your eyes follow his, that you read his soul, that you see all its changes in his countenance, that you anticipate his wishes, that you smile in his smile, and are sad in his sadness, and are downcast when he is vexed, and rejoice in his successes? To watch for Christ is a feeling such as all these.

PS, iv, 22

November 6

We are destined to come before Him; nay, and to come before Him in judgment; and that on our first meeting; and that suddenly. We are not merely to be rewarded or punished, we are to be judged. Recompense is to come upon our actions, not by a mere general provision or course of nature, as it does at present, but from the Lawgiver Himself in person. We have to stand before His righteous Presence, and that one by one. One by one we shall have to endure His holy and searching eye. At present we are in a world of shadows. What we see is not substantial. Suddenly it will be rent in twain and vanish away, and our Maker will appear. And then, I say, that first appearance will be nothing less than a personal intercourse between the Creator and every creature. He will look on us, while we look on Him.

PS, v, 1

November 7

The sight of Him will kindle in thy heart
All tender, gracious, reverential thoughts.
Thou wilt be sick with love, and yearn for Him,
And feel as though thou couldst but pity Him,
That one so sweet should e'er have placed Himself
At disadvantage such, as to be used
So vilely by a being so vile as thee.
There is a pleading in His pensive eyes
Will pierce thee to the quick, and trouble thee.
And thou wilt hate and loathe thyself; for, though
Now sinless, thou wilt feel that thou hast sinn'd,
As never thou didst feel; and wilt desire
To slink away, and hide thee from His sight:
And yet wilt have a longing aye to dwell
Within the beauty of His countenance.
And these two pains, so counter and so keen, –
The longing for Him, when thou seest Him not;
The shame of self at thought of seeing Him, –
Will be thy veriest, sharpest purgatory.

VV, 'Dream of Gerontius'

November 8

Appearing before God, and dwelling in His presence ... would seem to require ... a special preparation of thought and affection, such as will enable us to endure His countenance, and to hold communion with Him as we ought. Nay, and, it may be, a preparation of the soul itself for His presence, just as the bodily eye must be exercised in order to bear the full light of day, or the bodily frame in order to bear exposure to the air ... The Gospel Covenant is intended, among its other purposes, to prepare us for this future glorious and wonderful destiny, the sight of God, – a destiny which, if not most glorious, will be most terrible. And in the worship and service of Almighty God, which Christ and His Apostles have left to us, we are vouchsafed means, both moral and mystical, of approaching God, and gradually learning to bear the sight of Him.

PS, v, 1

November 9

Dedication of the Lateran basilica, Feast

Stability and permanence are, perhaps, the especial ideas which a church brings before the mind ... It represents to us its eternity. It is the witness of Him who is the beginning and the ending, the first and the last; it is the token and emblem of "Jesus Christ, the same yesterday, today, and for ever;"

PS, vi, 19

November 10

Saint Leo the Great, pope and doctor, Memorial

If we wish to express the sacred Mystery of the Incarnation accurately, we should rather say that God is man, than that man is God. Not that the latter proposition is not altogether Catholic in its wording, but the former expresses the *history* of the Economy, (if I may so call it,) and confines our Lord's personality to His divine nature, making His manhood an adjunct; whereas to say that man is God, does the contrary of both of these, – leads us to consider Him a man primarily and personally, with some vast and unknown dignity superadded, and that acquired of course after His coming into existence as man.

Ess., i, 2.3

November 11

Saint Martin of Tours, bishop, Memorial

Before Martin was a Bishop, while he was near St. Hilary at Poictiers, a certain Catechumen, who lived in his monastery, died of a fever, in Martin's absence, without baptism. On his return, the Saint went by himself into the cell where the body lay, threw himself upon it, prayed, and then raising himself with his eyes fixed on it, patiently waited his restoration, which took place before the end of two hours ... At another time, on his giving orders for cutting down a pine to which idolatrous honour was paid, a heathen said, "If thou hast confidence in thy God, let us hew the tree, and do thou receive it as it falls; if thy Lord is with thee, thou wilt escape harm." Martin accepted the condition, and when the tree was falling upon him, made the sign of the cross; the tree reeled round and fell on the other side. This miracle converted the vast multitude who were spectators of it.

Mir., 2.3

November 12

Saint Josaphat, bishop and martyr, Memorial

A political body cannot exist without government, and the larger is the body the more concentrated must the government be. If the whole of Christendom is to form one Kingdom, one head is essential; at least this is the experience of eighteen hundred years. As the Church grew into form, so did the power of the Pope develop; and wherever the Pope has been renounced, decay and division have been the consequence. We know of no other way of preserving the *Sacramentum Unitatis*, but a centre of unity.

Dev., 4.3

November 13

Love ... is the life of those who know not an external world, but who worship God as manifested within them. Such a life however can last but a little while on earth. The eyes see and the reason embraces a lower world, sun, moon, stars, and earth, and men, and all that man does or makes; and this external world does not speak of God upon the face of it. It shows as if it were itself God, and an object of worship, or at least it becomes the creature of a usurper, who has made himself "the god of this world." We are at once forced to reflect, reason, decide, and act; for we are between two, the inward voice speaking one thing within us, and the world speaking another without us; the world tempting, and the Spirit whispering warnings. Hence faith becomes necessary; in other words, God has most mercifully succoured us in this contest, by speaking not only in our hearts, but through the sensible world; and this Voice we call revelation. God has overruled this world of sense, and put a word in its mouth, and bid it prophesy of Him. And thus there are two voices even in the external world; the voice of the tempter calling us to fall down and worship him, and he will give us all; and the voice of God, speaking in aid of the voice in our hearts: and as love is that which hears the voice within us, so faith is that which hears the voice without us; and as love worships God within the shrine, faith discerns Him in the world; and as love is the life of God in the solitary soul, faith is the guardian of love in our intercourse with men; and, while faith ministers to love, love is that which imparts to faith its praise and excellence.

PS, iv, 21

November 14

As the essence of all religion is authority and obedience, so the distinction between natural religion and revealed lies in this, that the one has a subjective authority, and the other an objective. Revelation consists in the manifestation of the Invisible Divine Power, or in the substitution of the voice of a Lawgiver for the voice of conscience. The supremacy of conscience is the essence of natural religion; the supremacy of Apostle, or Pope, or Church, or Bishop, is the essence of revealed.

Dev., 2.2

November 15

Saint Albert the Great, bishop and doctor, Optional Memorial

While we are men, we cannot help, to a great extent, being Aristotelians, for the great Master does but analyze the thoughts, feelings, views, and opinions of human kind. He has told us the meaning of our own words and ideas, before we were born. In many subject-matters, to think correctly, is to think like Aristotle; and we are his disciples whether we will or no, though we may not know it.

Idea, 1.5

November 16

Saint Margaret of Scotland or Saint Gertrude the Great, virgin, Optional Memorial

The office of self-examination lies rather in detecting what is bad in us than in ascertaining what is good. No harm can follow from contemplating our sins, so that we keep Christ before us, and attempt to overcome them; such a review of self will but lead to repentance and faith.

PS, ii, 14

November 17

Saint Elizabeth of Hungary, religious, Memorial

True repentance cannot be without the thought of God; it has the thought of God, for it seeks Him; and it seeks Him, because it is quickened with love; and even sorrow must have a sweetness, if love be in it. For what is to repent but to surrender ourselves to God for pardon or punishment; as loving His presence for its own sake, and accounting chastisement from Him better than rest and peace from the world?

PS, v, 22

November 18

Dedication of the basilicas of Saints Peter and Paul, Apostles, Optional Memorial

How do we glorify God in religious houses or churches? In making them *devotional*. No matter what architecture ... *devotional* is the end, towards God and towards men.

SN, July 2, 1871

November 19

God's works are like each other, not different; if, then, the Gospel is from God, and the Jewish religion was from God, and the various heathen religions in their first origin were from God, it is not wonderful, rather it is natural, that they should have in many ways a resemblance one with another. And, accordingly, that the Gospel is in certain points like the religions which preceded it, is but an argument that "God is One, and that there is none other but He."

PS, v, 12

November 20

The old saws of nations, the majestic precepts of philosophy, the luminous maxims of law, the oracles of individual wisdom, the traditionary rules of truth, justice, and religion, even though imbedded in the corruption, or alloyed with the pride, of the world, betoken His original agency, and His long-suffering presence. Even where there is habitual rebellion against Him, or profound far-spreading social depravity, still the undercurrent, or the heroic outburst, of natural virtue, as well as the yearnings of the heart after what it has not, and its presentiment of its true remedies, are to be ascribed to the Author of all good. Anticipations or reminiscences of His glory haunt the mind of the self-sufficient sage, and of the pagan devotee; His writing is upon the wall, whether of the Indian fane, or of the porticoes of Greece.

Idea, 1.3

November 21

Presentation of the Blessed Virgin Mary, Memorial

Eve ... was the first-fruits of God's beautiful creation. She was the type of all beauty; but alas! she represented the world also in its fragility. She stayed not in her original creation. Mary comes as a second and holier Eve, having the grace of indefectibility and the gift of perseverance from the first, and teaching us how to use God's gifts without abusing them.

SN, May 1, 1851

November 22

Saint Cecilia, Memorial

Music ... is the expression of ideas greater and more profound than any in the visible world.

Idea, 1.4

November 23

Saint Clement I, pope and martyr, or Saint Columban, religious, Optional Memorial

The visible world still remains without its divine interpretation; Holy Church in her sacraments and her hierarchical appointments, will remain, even to the end of the world, after all but a symbol of those heavenly facts which fill eternity. Her mysteries are but the expressions in human language of truths to which the human mind is unequal.

Apo., 1

November 24

Saint Andre Dung Lac and companions, martyrs, Memorial

This is what Christianity has done in the world; such is the result of Christian teaching; viz., to elicit, foster, mature the seeds of heaven which lie hid in the earth, to multiply (if it may be said) images of Christ, which, though they be few, are worth all else that is among men, and are an ample recompense and "a crown of rejoicing" for

Apostles and Evangelists "in the presence of our Lord Jesus Christ at His coming." (1 Thess. i. 19.)

PS, iv, 10

November 25

Saint Catherine of Alexandria, Optional Memorial

If Christians are to live together, they will pray together; and united prayer is necessarily of an intercessory character, as being offered for each other and for the whole, and for self as one of the whole. In proportion, then, as unity is an especial Gospel-duty, so does Gospel-prayer partake of a social character; and Intercession becomes a token of the existence of a Church Catholic.

PS, iii, 24

November 26

The great mystery is, not that evil has no end, but that it had a beginning.

GA, 10.2

November 27

If I looked into a mirror, and did not see my face, I should have the sort of feeling which actually comes upon me, when I look into this living busy world, and see no reflexion of its Creator ... Were it not for this voice, speaking so clearly in my conscience and my heart, I should be an atheist, or a pantheist, or a polytheist when I looked into the world.

APVS, 5

November 28

Almighty God, Thou art the One Infinite Fulness. From eternity Thou art the One and only absolute and most all-sufficient seat and proper abode of all conceivable best attributes, and of all, which are many more, which cannot be conceived. I hold this as a matter of reason, though my imagination starts from it. I hold it firmly and absolutely, though it is the most difficult of all mysteries.

I hold it from the actual experience of Thy blessings and mercies towards me, the evidences of Thy awful Being and attributes, brought home continually to my reason, beyond the power of doubting or disputing. I hold it from that long and intimate familiarity with it, so that it is part of my rational nature to hold it; because I am so constituted and made up upon the idea of it, as a keystone, that not to hold it would be to break my mind to pieces. I hold it from that intimate perception of it in my conscience, as a fact present to me, that I feel it as easy to deny my own personality as the personality of God, and have lost my grounds for believing that I exist myself, if I deny existence to Him. I hold it because I could not bear to be without Thee, O my Lord and Life, because I look for blessings beyond thought by being with Thee. I hold it from the terror of being left in this wild world without stay or protection. I hold it from humble love to Thee, from delight in Thy glory and exaltation, from my desire that Thou shouldst be great and the only great one. I hold it for Thy sake, and because I love to think of Thee as so glorious, perfect, and beautiful. There is one God, and none other but He.

MD, 3.21

November 29

We are immortal spirits, independent of time and space, and that this life is but a sort of outward stage, on which we act for a time, and which is only sufficient and only intended to answer the purpose of trying whether we will serve God or no. We should consider ourselves to be in this world in no fuller sense than players in any game are in the game; and life to be a sort of dream, as detached and as different from our real eternal existence, as a dream differs from waking; a serious dream, indeed, as affording a means of judging us, yet in itself a kind of shadow without substance, a scene set before us, in which we seem to be, and in which it is our duty to act just as if all we saw had a truth and reality, because all that meets us influences us and our destiny. The regenerate soul is taken into communion with Saints and Angels, and its "life is hid with Christ in God" (Col. iii. 3.); it has a place in God's court, and is not of this world, – looking into this world as a spectator might look at some show or pageant, except when called from time to time to take a part. And while it obeys the instinct of the senses, it does so for God's sake, and it submits itself to things of time so far as to be brought to perfection by them, that, when the veil is withdrawn and it sees itself to be, where it ever has been, in God's kingdom, it may be found worthy to enjoy it.

PS, iv, 14

November 30

Saint Andrew the Apostle, Feast

St. Andrew was the first convert among the Apostles; he was especially in our Lord's confidence; thrice is he described as introducing others to Him; [but] he is little known in history, while the place of dignity and the name of highest renown have been allotted to his brother Simon, whom he was the means of bringing to the knowledge of his Saviour ... Those men are not necessarily the most useful men in their generation, not the most favoured by God, who make the most noise in the world, and who seem to be principals in the great changes and events recorded in history ... His marvellous providence works beneath a veil, which speaks but an untrue language; and to see Him who is the Truth and the Life, we must stoop underneath it, and so in our turn hide ourselves from the world.

PS, ii, 1

December

December 1

Year after year, as it passes, brings us the same warnings again and again, and none perhaps more impressive than those with which it comes to us at this season. The very frost and cold, rain and gloom, which now befall us, forebode the last dreary days of the world, and in religious hearts raise the thought of them. The year is worn out: spring, summer, autumn, each in turn, have brought their gifts and done their utmost; but they are over, and the end is come ... Thus the soul is cast forward upon the future, and in proportion as its conscience is clear and its perception keen and true, does it rejoice solemnly that "the night is far spent, the day is at hand," that there are "new heavens and a new earth" to come, though the former are failing; nay, rather that, because they are failing, it will "soon see the King in His beauty," and "behold the land which is very far off." These are feelings for holy men in winter and in age, waiting, in some dejection perhaps, but with comfort on the whole, and calmly though earnestly, for the Advent of Christ.

PS, v, 1

December 2

While the times wax old, and the colours of earth fade, and the voice of song is brought low, and all kindreds of the earth can but wail and lament, the sons of God lift up their heads, for their salvation draweth nigh. Nature fails, the sun shines not, and the moon is dim, the stars fall from heaven, and the foundations of the round world shake; but the Altar's light burns ever brighter; there are sights there which the many cannot see, and all above the tumults of earth the command is heard to show forth the Lord's death, and the promise that the Lord is coming.

PS, vii, 11

December 3

Saint Francis Xavier, priest, Memorial

The view, which animated, first Christ Himself, then all His Apostles, and St. Paul in particular, [was] to preach to all, in order to succeed with some ... And such is the office of the Church in every nation where she sojourns; she attempts much, she expects and promises little.

PS, iv, 10

December 4

Saint John Damascene, priest and doctor, Optional Memorial

When the Eternal Son came on earth in our flesh, men saw their invisible Maker and Judge. He showed Himself no longer through the mere powers of nature, or the maze of human affairs, but in our own likeness to Him.

PS, iii, 9

December 5

"The Word was made flesh;" by which is meant, not that He selected some particular existing man and dwelt in him ... but that He became what He was not before, that He took into His own Infinite Essence man's nature itself in all its completeness, creating a soul and body, and, at the moment of creation, making them His own, so that they never were other than His, never existed by themselves or except as in Him, being properties or attributes of Him (to use defective words) as really as His divine goodness, or His eternal Sonship, or His perfect likeness to the Father. And, while thus adding a new nature to Himself, He did not in any respect cease to be what He was before. How was that possible? All the while He was on earth, when He was conceived, when He was born, when He was tempted, on the cross, in the grave, and now at God's right hand – all the time through, He was the Eternal and Unchangeable Word, the Son of God. The flesh which He had assumed was but the instrument through which He acted for and towards us.

PS, iii, 12

December 6

Saint Nicholas, bishop, Optional Memorial

The heavenly gift of the Spirit fixes the eyes of our mind upon the Divine Author of our salvation. By nature we are blind and carnal; but the Holy Ghost by whom we are new-born, reveals to us the God of mercies, and bids us recognise and adore Him as our Father with a true heart.

PS, ii, 19

December 7

Saint Ambrose, bishop and doctor, Memorial

As Athanasius was the great champion of the Catholic Faith, while the Arians were in the ascendant; so Basil and Gregory in the East, and Ambrose in the West, were the chief instruments of Providence in repairing and strengthening its bulwarks, by word, writing, and deed, when the fury of their assaults was spent.

HS, ii, CF, 1

December 8

Immaculate Conception of the Blessed Virgin Mary, Solemnity

If Eve was raised above human nature by that indwelling moral gift which we call grace, is it rash to say that Mary had even a greater grace? ... And if Eve had this supernatural inward gift given her from the first moment of her personal existence, is it possible to deny that Mary too had this gift from the very first moment of her personal existence? ... She had this special privilege, in order to fit her to become the Mother of her and our Redeemer, to fit her mentally, spiritually for it; so that, by the aid of the first grace, she might so grow in grace, that, when the Angel came and her Lord was at hand, she might be "full of grace," prepared as far as a creature could be prepared, to receive Him into her bosom.

Diff., ii, 3

December 9

Saint Juan Diego

Since Faith is the characteristic of all Christians, a peasant may take the same view of human affairs in detail as a philosopher.

US, 14

December 10

Reasoning ... or the exercise of Reason, is a living spontaneous energy within us, not an art ... All men have a reason, but not all men can give a reason.

US, 13

December 11

Saint Damasus I, pope, Optional Memorial

Incomprehensible it is, and we can but adore, when we hear that the Almighty Being, of whom I have been speaking, "who inhabiteth eternity," has taken flesh and blood of a Virgin's veins, lain in a Virgin's womb, been suckled at a Virgin's breast, been obedient to human parents, worked at a humble trade, been despised by His own, been buffeted and scourged by His creatures, been nailed hand and foot to a Cross, and has died a malefactor's death; and that now, under the form of Bread, He should lie upon our Altars, and suffer Himself to be hidden in a small tabernacle!

Most incomprehensible, but still, while the thought overwhelms our imagination, it also overpowers our heart; it is the most subduing, affecting, piercing thought which can be pictured to us. It thrills through us, and draws our tears, and abases us, and melts us into love and affection, when we dwell upon it. O most tender and compassionate Lord!

Mix., 13

December 12

Our Lady of Guadalupe, Optional Memorial

Thy very face and form, dear Mother, speak to us of the Eternal; not like earthly beauty, dangerous to look upon, but like the morning star, which is thy emblem, bright and musical, breathing purity, telling of heaven, and infusing peace. O harbinger of day! O hope of the pilgrim! lead us still as thou hast led; in the dark night, across the bleak wilderness, guide us on to our Lord Jesus, guide us home.

Mix., 17

December 13

Saint Lucy of Syracuse, virgin and martyr, Memorial

I adore Thee, O my God, as the true and only Light! From Eternity to Eternity, before any creature was, when Thou wast alone, alone but not solitary, for Thou hast ever been Three in One, Thou wast the Infinite Light. There was none to see Thee but Thyself. The Father saw that Light in the Son, and the Son in the Father. Such as Thou wast in the beginning, such Thou art now. Most separate from all creatures in this Thy uncreated Brightness. Most glorious, most beautiful. Thy attributes are so many separate and resplendent colours, each as perfect in its own purity and grace as if it were the sole and highest perfection. Nothing created is more than the very shadow of Thee ... I cannot even look upon the sun, and what is this but a base material emblem of Thee? How should I endure to look even on an Angel? and how could I look upon Thee and live? If I were placed in the illumination of Thy countenance, I should shrink up like the grass. O most gracious God, who shall approach Thee, being so glorious, yet how can I keep from Thee.

MD, 3.7.3

December 14

Saint John of the Cross, priest and doctor, Memorial

Let me ever hold communion with Thee, my hidden, but my living God. Thou art in my innermost heart. Thou art the life of my life. Every breath I breathe, every thought of my mind, every good desire of my heart, is from the presence within me of the unseen God.

MD, 3.7.2

December 15

What, then, is meant by the "Son of God?" It is meant that our Lord is the very or true Son of God, that is, His Son by nature. We are but *called* the sons of God – we are adopted to be sons – but our Lord and Saviour is the Son of God, really and by birth, and He alone is such … In that He is the Son of God, He must be whatever God is, all-holy, all-wise, all-powerful, all-good, eternal, infinite; yet since there is only one God, He must be at the same time not separate from God, but ever one with and in Him, one indivisibly; so that it would be as idle language to speak of Him as separated in essence from His Father, as to say that our reason, or intellect, or will, was separate from our minds – as rash and profane language to deny to the Father His Only-begotten Word, in whom He has ever delighted, as to deny His Wisdom or Goodness, or Power, which also have been in and with Him from everlasting.

PS, iii, 12

December 16

When we confess God as Omnipotent only, we have gained but a half-knowledge of Him: His is an Omnipotence which can at the same time swathe Itself in infirmity and can become the captive of Its own creatures. He has, if I may so speak, the incomprehensible power of even making Himself weak. We must know Him by His names, Emmanuel and Jesus, to know Him perfectly.

OS, 6

December 17

Thou askest us to love Thee, O my God, and Thou art Thyself Love. There was one attribute of Thine which Thou didst exercise from eternity, and that was Love. We hear of no exercise of Thy power whilst Thou wast alone, nor of Thy justice before there were creatures on their trial; nor of Thy wisdom before the acts and works of Thy Providence; but from eternity Thou didst love, for Thou art not only One but Three. The Father loved from eternity His only begotten Son, and the Son returned to Him an equal love. And the Holy Ghost is that love in substance, wherewith the Father and the Son love one another. This, O Lord, is Thine ineffable and special blessedness. It is love.

MD, 3.10

December 18

As the Son was God, so on the other hand was the Son suitably made man; it belonged to Him to have the Father's perfections, it became Him to assume a servant's form ... He was a Son both before His incarnation, and, by a second mystery, after it. From eternity He had been the Only-begotten in the bosom of the Father; and when He came on earth, this essential relation to the Father remained unaltered; still, He was a Son, when in the form of a servant, – still performing the will of the Father, as His Father's Word and Wisdom, manifesting His Father's glory and accomplishing His Father's purposes.

PS, vi, 5

December 19

Having clothed Himself with a created essence, He made it the instrument of His humiliation; He acted in it, He obeyed and suffered through it ... That Eternal Power, which, till then, had thought and acted as God, began to think and act as a man, with all man's faculties, affections, and imperfections, sin excepted.

Before He came on earth, He was infinitely above joy and grief, fear and anger, pain and heaviness; but afterwards all these properties and many more were His as fully as they are ours.

PS, iii, 12

December 20

Christ ... took our nature, when He would redeem it; He redeemed it by making it suffer in His own Person; He purified it, by making it pure in His own Person. He first sanctified it in Himself, made it righteous, made it acceptable to God, submitted it to an expiatory passion, and then He imparted it to us. He took it, consecrated it, broke it, and said, "Take, and divide it among yourselves."

PS, v, 9

December 21

Saint Peter Canisius, priest and doctor, Optional Memorial

"*Tota* pulchra es, Maria!" Nothing of the deformity of sin was ever hers. Thus she differs from all saints. There have been great missionaries, confessors, bishops, doctors, pastors. They have done great works, and have taken with them numberless converts or penitents to heaven. They have suffered much, and have a superabundance of merits to show. But Mary in this way resembles her Divine Son, viz., that, as He, being God, is separate by holiness from all creatures, so she is separate from all Saints and Angels, as being "*full of grace.*"

MD, 1.1.7

December 22

As speech is the organ of human society, and the means of human civilization, so is prayer the instrument of divine fellowship and divine training.

PS, iv, 15

December 23

Saint John of Kanty, priest, Optional Memorial

Whereas He was God from everlasting, as the Only-begotten of the Father, He took on Him the thoughts, affections, and infirmities of man, thereby, through the fulness of His Divine Nature, to raise those thoughts and affections, and destroy those infirmities, that so, by God's becoming man, men, through brotherhood with Him, might in the end become as gods.

PS, v, 9

December 24

The world of spirits, though unseen, is present; present, not future, not distant. It is not above the sky, it is not beyond the grave; it is now and here; the kingdom of God is among us ... and, as it is now hidden, so in due season it shall be revealed. Men think that they are lords of the world, and may do as they will. They think this earth their property, and its movements in their power; whereas it has other lords besides them, and is the scene of a higher conflict than they are capable of conceiving. It contains Christ's little ones whom they despise, and His Angels whom they disbelieve; and these at length shall take possession of it and be manifested ... At the appointed time there will be a "manifestation of the sons of God," and the hidden saints "shall shine out as the sun in the kingdom of their Father." When the Angels appeared to the shepherds, it was a sudden appearance, – "*Suddenly* there was with the Angel a multitude of the heavenly host." How wonderful a sight! The night had before that seemed just like any other night ... They were keeping watch over their sheep; they were watching the night as it passed. The stars moved on – it was midnight. They had no idea of such a thing when the Angel appeared. Such are the power and virtue hidden in things which are seen, and at God's will they are manifested ... They will be manifested for ever when Christ comes at the Last Day "in the glory of His Father with the holy Angels." Then this world will fade away and the other world will shine forth.

PS, iv, 13

December 25

Christmas

The Son of God and we are of one; He has become "the firstborn of every creature;" He has taken our nature, and in and through it He sanctifies us ... This is the wonderful economy of grace, or mystery of godliness, which should be before our minds at all times, but especially at this season, when the Most Holy took upon Him our flesh of "a pure Virgin," "by the operation of the Holy Ghost, without spot of sin, to make us clean from all sin" ... He it was who created the worlds; He it was who interposed of old time in the affairs of the world, and showed Himself to be a living and observant God, whether men thought of Him or not. Yet this great God condescended to come down on earth from His heavenly throne, and to be born into His own world; showing Himself as the Son of God in a new and second sense, in a created nature, as well as in His eternal substance ... He who "hath made of one blood all nations of men," so that in the sin of one all sinned, and in the death of one all died, He came in that very nature of Adam, in order to communicate to us that nature as it is in His Person, that "our sinful bodies might be made clean by His Body, and our souls washed through His most precious Blood;" to make us partakers of the Divine nature; to sow the seed of eternal life in our hearts; and to raise us from "the corruption that is in the world through lust," to that immaculate purity and that fulness of grace which is in Him. He who is the first principle and pattern of all things, came to be the beginning and pattern of human kind, the firstborn of the whole creation. He, who is the everlasting Light, became the Light of men; He, who is the Life from eternity, became the Life of a race dead in sin; He, who is the Word of God, came to be a spiritual Word, "dwelling richly in our hearts," an "engrafted Word, which is able to save our souls;" He, who is the co-equal Son of the Father, came to be the Son of God in our flesh, that He might raise us also to the adoption of sons, and might be first among many brethren.

Let us at this season approach Him with awe and love, in whom resides all perfection, and from whom we are allowed to gain it. Let us come to the Sanctifier to be sanctified ... May each Christmas, as it comes, find us more and more like Him, who as at this time became a little child for our sake, more simple-minded, more humble, more holy, more affectionate, more resigned, more happy, more full of God.

PS, v, 7

December 26

St Stephen, the first martyr, Feast

When the blood of Stephen was shed, Saul, then a young man, was standing by, "consenting unto his death," and "kept the raiment of them that slew him." (Acts xxii. 20.) Two speeches are recorded of the Martyr in his last moments; one, in which he prayed that God would pardon his murderers, – the other his witness, that he saw the heavens opened, and Jesus on God's right hand. His prayer was wonderfully answered. Stephen saw his Saviour; the next vision of that Saviour to mortal man was vouchsafed to that very young man, even Saul, who shared in his murder and his intercession.

Strange indeed it was; and what would have been St. Stephen's thoughts could he have known it! The prayers of righteous men avail much. The first Martyr had power with God to raise up the greatest Apostle. Such was the honour put upon the first-fruits of those sufferings upon which the Church was entering. Thus from the beginning the blood of the Martyrs was the seed of the Church.

PS, ii, 9

December 27

Saint John the Apostle and evangelist, Feast

There are [Saints] ... who are so absorbed in the divine life, that they seem, even while they are in the flesh, to have no part in earth or in human nature; but to think, speak, and act under views, affections, and motives simply supernatural. If they love others, it is simply because they love God, and because man is the object either of His compassion, or of His praise. If they rejoice, it is in what is unseen; if they feel interest, it is in what is unearthly; if they speak, it is almost with the voice of Angels; if they eat or drink, it is almost of Angels' food alone, – for it is recorded in their histories, that for weeks they have fed on nothing else but that Heavenly

Bread which is the proper sustenance of the soul. Such we may suppose to have been St. John.

OS, 7

December 28

Holy Innocents, martyrs, Feast

This seems to have been man's happiness in Paradise, not to think about himself or to be conscious of himself. Such, too … seems to be the state of children. They do not reflect upon themselves. Such, too, seems to be the state of those orders of Angels whose life is said to consist in contemplation – for what is contemplation but a resting in the thought of God to the forgetfulness of self?

PS, viii, 18

December 29

Saint Thomas Becket, bishop and martyr, Optional Memorial

His dispensations move forward in an equable uniform way, like circles expanding about one centre; – the greater good to come being, not indeed the same as the past good, but nevertheless resembling it, as a substance resembles its type. In the past we see the future as if in miniature and outline. Indeed how can it be otherwise? seeing that all goods are but types and shadows of God Himself the Giver, and are like each other because they are like Him.

PS, v, 8

December 30

God beholds thee individually, whoever thou art. He "calls thee by thy name." He sees thee, and understands thee, as He made thee. He knows what is in thee, all thy own peculiar feelings and thoughts, thy dispositions and likings, thy strength and thy weakness. He views thee in thy day of rejoicing, and thy day of sorrow. He sympathises in thy hopes and thy temptations. He interests Himself in all thy anxieties and remembrances, all the risings and fallings of thy spirit. He has numbered the very hairs of thy head and the cubits of thy stature. He compasses thee round and bears thee in his arms; He takes thee up and sets thee down. He notes thy very countenance, whether smiling or in tears, whether healthful or sickly. He looks tenderly upon thy hands and thy feet; He hears thy voice, the beating of thy heart, and thy very breathing. Thou dost not love thyself better than He loves thee. Thou canst not shrink from pain more than He dislikes thy bearing it; and if He puts it on thee, it is as thou would put it on thyself, if thou art wise, for a greater good afterwards. Thou art not only His creature (though for the very sparrows He has a care, and pitied the "much cattle" of Nineveh), thou art man redeemed and sanctified, His adopted son, favoured with a portion of that glory and blessedness which flows from Him everlastingly unto the Only-begotten. Thou art chosen to be His, even above thy fellows who dwell in the East and South. Thou wast one of those for whom Christ offered up His last prayer, and sealed it with His precious blood.

PS, iii, 9

December 31

Saint Sylvester I, pope, Optional Memorial

The very glories of nature, the sun, moon, and stars, and the richness and the beauty of the earth, are as types and figures witnessing and teaching the invisible things of God. All that we see is destined one day to burst forth into a heavenly bloom, and to be transfigured into immortal glory. Heaven at present is out of sight, but in due time, as snow melts and discovers what it lay upon, so will this visible creation fade away before those greater splendours which are behind it, and on which at present it depends. In that day shadows will retire, and the substance show itself. The sun will grow pale and be lost in the sky, but it will be before the radiance of Him whom it does but image, the Sun of Righteousness, with healing on His wings, who will come forth in visible form, as a bridegroom out of his chamber, as His perishable type decays. The stars which surround it will be replaced by Saints and Angels circling His throne. Above and below, the clouds of the air, the trees of the field, the waters of the great deep will be found impregnated with the forms of everlasting spirits, the servants of God which do His pleasure. And our own mortal bodies will then be found in like manner to contain within them an inner man, which will then receive its due proportions, as the soul's harmonious organ, instead of that gross mass of flesh and blood which sight and touch are sensible of. For this glorious manifestation the whole creation is at present in travail, earnestly desiring that it may be accomplished in its season.

PS, iv, 14